PALM SPRINGS

Including Joshua Tree and Death Valley National Parks

LIZ HAMILL SCOTT

Contents

PALM SPRINGS

THE DESERTS

Cosmopolitan Palm Springs and its many outlying towns are havens for wealthy residents of northern climates who come down each winter to escape the cold. Great golf and wonderful day spas are hallmarks of Palm Springs proper, Rancho Mirage, Palm Desert, and Indian Wells.

But beauty can be harsh, and nowhere is this more true than in the California deserts. Only a few miles away from Palm Springs, Joshua Tree National Monument sprawls across the desert landscape, connecting two major California desert climates—the Mojave Desert and the lower Colorado Desert. Joshua Tree is easier to access from the Los Angeles area, featuring the strange shapes of the plant that is its namesake. North, the seemingly endless Mojave stretches across the state, offering hiking trails, preserve areas, ghost towns, and even camping for the hardy traveler.

Death Valley hugs the Nevada border at the east side of the state and its barrenness is legendary. In truth, Death Valley is misnamed. This vast forbidding landscape encompasses a wealth of life; a vast variety of plants, animals, birds, and even fish call the Valley home. Spring is the best time to experience this contradiction, when an astonishing bloom of wildflowers brightens the desert landscape.

The southernmost desert park of California is Anza-Borrego State Park. The biggest of all California's state parks, Anza-Borrego is part of the Colorado Desert region and home to its diverse array of wildlife. From ocotillo fields to palm oases to profuse spring wildflower blooms, the beauty of this desert's gardens

© LANCE SCOTT

PARK OFF
PAVEMENT

ELEVATION
SEA LEVEL

HIGHLIGHTS

◖ Palm Springs Aerial Tramway: For a stunning view of Palm Springs and the San Jacinto Mountains, nothing beats an exhilarating ride up the Aerial Tramway, which zips up 2.5 miles in about 10 minutes and provides a 360° view of the valley below (page 9).

◖ Oasis of Mara: No, it's not a mirage! The lush Oasis of Mara, accessible via a 0.5-mile nature loop, provides an up-close glimpse into the history and ecology of Joshua Tree National Park (page 26).

◖ Keys View: This panoramic view is one of the best in Joshua Tree. Pick a clear day to take in the vista from Palm Springs all the way out to the Salton Sea (page 29).

◖ Scotty's Castle: Don't miss touring the only private mansion built in Death Valley. This grand home, albeit unfinished, provides an entertaining Gold Rush–era history to the region (page 38).

◖ Badwater Basin: Take a walk along the esoteric landscape of this dried-out lakebed, situated at the lowest elevation in the Western Hemisphere (page 40).

◖ Artist's Palette: Nature is the ultimate artist here, where a combination of minerals paints the badlands in brilliant colors. Time your visit at sunset, when the fading light washes the already colorful mountains in glistening gold (page 40).

◖ Borrego Palm Canyon: This canyon provides the best overview of Anza Borrego flora and fauna. An easy three-mile loop takes visitors from sandy desert to shady palm groves with interpretive stops along the way (page 53).

LOOK FOR ◖ TO FIND RECOMMENDED SIGHTS, ACTIVITIES, DINING, AND LODGING.

rivals any in the world. Nearby, the former mining town of Julian offers a taste of Southern California gold rush history.

PLANNING YOUR TIME
Palm Springs makes a great weekend getaway or a relaxing spot to kick back for a whole season—just ask the thousands of Californians who maintain vacation condos here or are regulars at the coolest hotels. In the summertime, many Los Angelenos who want to escape the summer fog at the coast come out to the desert for some serious heat and swimming pool time. In the winter, mild temperatures lure Palm Springs visitors out for easy day trips to Joshua Tree.

Death Valley makes another great weekend destination, as does Anza-Borrego. You can pick lodgings right in the center of these deserts, then spend your time on Saturday and

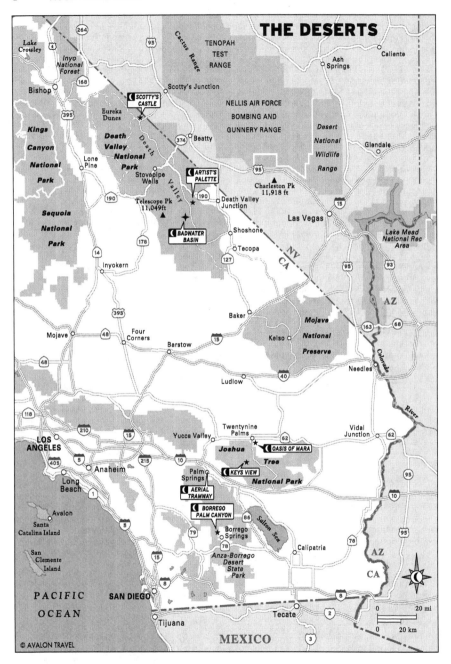

THE DESERTS

Sunday driving to the major sights and picking a few spectacular hikes before heading out on Sunday afternoon.

If you're a true desert rat and want to do a tour of all California's major deserts, plan at least a week to 10 days. The parks cover broad swaths of California's southern regions, and the distances between them can take hours to drive, especially along some of the more interesting back roads. Then you'll want to spend at least a day or two exploring within each desert. Leaving yourself enough time to enjoy the diverse ecosystems and unique sights will make the trip worthwhile.

HISTORY

The history of the deserts of California is actually the geological history of the American continent. Two major deserts collide in California: the high-altitude Mojave to the north and the lower-lying Colorado in the southeast.

The most famous desert park in California, Death Valley, has its own story. Death Valley's formation began at least two billion years ago,

and its landscape has been evolving ever since. Lakes have formed and dried up in its famous below-sea-level basin to the south, and recent volcanic activity is evident at the north end of the valley. Even as you wander around, the desert is changing all around you. Wind, gravity, and even water erode the valley's walls, shift its dunes, and create a new and different place every single day.

At heart, Palm Springs is a Hollywood town. As the movie industry heated up in the Los Angeles Basin, the industry had to find someplace to shoot desert and "Old West" locations. And the stars started seeking someplace to escape Hollywood and enjoy themselves on their own time. In the Golden Age of Hollywood (the 1930s, '40s, and '50s), film crews crowded into Palm Springs and stars built weekend homes with sparkling swimming pools. Today, many of the original 1940s and '50s inns that once housed producers and film crews now open their doors to guests of the area, and architecture buffs come to tour the original mid-century modern mansions and villas.

Palm Springs

Palm Springs is a desert town with many faces. Some folks think of it as a wintertime snowbird retreat—that is, the spot where thousands of retired folks come to escape the harsh winter weather of their hometowns. To Hollywood star-followers, it's both a vacation haven for actors and a major on-location shooting site for many classic films of the 1940s and '50s. And for the young and vivacious gay crowd, it's a thriving and accepting town that's been known for its tolerance for more than five decades, complete with plenty of hot nightspots.

The Palm Springs area actually encompasses several medium-sized towns that have grown enough to bleed together into one sprawling urban area. Palm Springs proper maintains its status as the poshest and most happening place to be. As you drive south through Ranch Mirage, Palm Desert, Indian Wells, and down

to Indio, you'll find more residential communities and country clubs with clusters of mall-style shopping but no real historic downtown areas. By the time you get to Indio, the industrial part of the area begins to take over, and the only real tourist sights are the date farms.

SIGHTS
◖ Palm Springs Aerial Tramway

At first glance, Palm Springs doesn't seem like a spot where a gondola ride would be a big attraction. And yet, the Palm Springs Aerial Tramway (1 Tramway Rd., 760/325-1391, www.pstramway.com, Mon.–Fri. 10 A.M.–9:45 P.M., Sat.–Sun. 8 A.M.–9:45 P.M., adults $21.95, children 3–12 $14.95, seniors $19.95) draws both visitors and a surprising number of locals nearly every day of the year. The idea for the tramway was conceived by prominent and sweaty resident Francis Crocker in 1935. Crocker longed to visit the cool, snow-capped peak of Mount San Jacinto when the sun beat down mercilessly on the valley floor. It took nearly 30 years of wartime delays and political missteps to realize the dream, but in 1963 the structure was complete and the first visitors took a ride up to the peak of the 10,834-foot mountain. In 2000, the tramway was renovated, and now runs the biggest revolving cars operating in the world.

To take a ride on the tramway, you first drive up a winding road to the parking lots of the Valley Station. Purchase or pick up your tickets, then wait for your tram to depart. (Schedules vary based on season and weather conditions.)

You'll board the tram car and find a good place to stand on the circular metal platform, which can get fairly crowded. As the tram begins to climb, the platform revolves, letting passengers take in all the different views up and down the valley. The whole trip takes only 10 minutes as the tram ascends about 8,000 feet. When you get off the tram, you'll be in the Mountain Station, which includes a bar, a restaurant, a souvenir shop, and a visitors center for the surrounding Mount San Jacinto State Park (see *Sports and Recreation*).

But most folks head straight out the back door and into the park. In the wintertime, the park is usually covered by several feet of snow.

Locals bring their snowshoes, cross-country skis, sleds, and snow toys up on the tram (all of these are allowed in the car) for a fun few hours in the snow. The park creates a **Winter Adventure Center** (Thurs.–Fri. and Mon., 10 A.M.–4 P.M., Sat.–Sun. 8 A.M.–4 P.M., Nov.–Apr., ski package $21/day), a snow park with sled tracks, each winter. In the summertime when the snow is gone, those same locals take picnic supplies and walking sticks up to the mountain for a cool day's hiking and nature-loving.

Palm Springs Art Museum

Just a couple of blocks from the main drag, the Palm Springs Art Museum (101 Museum Dr., 760/322-4800, http://psmuseum.org, Tues.–Sun. 10 A.M.–5 P.M., Thurs. until 8 P.M., adults $12.50, children $5) shows off the finest modern art in a variety of media. From your first steps up to the museum entrance, which is flanked by a pair of large sculptures, you'll be ensconced in the forms and shapes of modern art. The museum's central permanent collection is a mix of Western and Native American fine art and crafts. From local artists and craftspeople as well as those from around the Western states, these pieces evoke the sense of space and beauty found in Palm Springs and beyond. Other permanent exhibits include an ever-changing array of modern glass sculpture and an almost-new installation by Patrick Dougherty. The Palm Springs Art Museum also hosts an endless parade of traveling shows and special exhibitions, from video installations to sculpture collections to photography.

Moorten Botanical Garden

Visitors who've come to the desert to learn and view the variety of desert wildlife will love the Moorten Botanical Garden (1701 S. Palm Canyon Dr., 760/327-6555, Mon.–Sat. 9 A.M.–4:30 P.M., Sun. 10 A.M.–4 P.M., adults $3, children $1.50). Set right near downtown, this charming garden specializes in cacti and succulents, growing over 3,000 varieties. The desert plants originate from all over the world, from South Africa and Madagascar to South America and much more locally in the Mojave and Sonora deserts of California. You can wander the outdoor gardens, then head inside to the "Cacterium," a greenhouse in which the more delicate (and less adapted to the Palm Springs locale) specimens thrive.

The Moorten gardens were created and expanded by Patricia and "Slim" Moorten; Slim was one of the original Keystone Cops. Today, their son Clark owns and operates the gardens. Be sure to say hi if you see him out working on his pride and joy.

The Living Desert

Do you prefer animal life to an endless parade of plants? Then head for The Living Desert (47900 Portola Ave., Palm Desert/Indian Wells, 760/346-5694, www.livingdesert.org, daily 9 A.M.–5 P.M., summer 8 A.M.–1 P.M., adults $12.50, children $7.50). The truth is you can visit a bunch more botanical gardens at The Living Desert. But you can also visit the animals—furry, scaly, feathered, and bald—that inhabit the world's great deserts. The Living Desert focuses primarily on the desert habitats of Africa and the Western United States. Some

ROBERT HOLMES / CALTOUR

desert bighorn sheep at The Living Desert

of the African natives, such as the gazelles and sand cats, are endangered species; others, like the meerkats, are stars of the small screen. The Discovery Center welcomes children of all ages, offering basic educational opportunities and interactive exhibits. The WaTuTu Village focuses on the lives of human natives of desert regions, and a somewhat incongruous but nonetheless impressive model train setup round out The Living Desert offerings.

Visitors can expect plenty of amenities at The Living Desert, including two café-style restaurants, two gift shops, and plenty of restrooms with baby-changing stations. The paved paths are wheelchair- and stroller-accessible. In addition, a number of shaded spots have water misters that cool off guests during the heat of summer.

Date Farms
In the south part of the urban region, groves of dates provide most of the United States' crop of the sweet Middle Eastern staple fruit. The **Oasis Date Farm** (59–111 Hwy. 111, Thermal, 800/827-8017, http://oasisdategardens.com, Mon.–Sat. 8 A.M.–5 P.M.) in the thriving metropolis of Thermal has a good-sized storefront and a demonstration "arbor" of date palms that visitors can walk around in. In the store, you can learn about the many different varieties of dates (interestingly, most dates originally come from Iraq) and taste almost all of them. You can buy whole dates, mixed boxes, and date candies. Over at the ice cream counter, the one thing you simply must try is the date shake—a super-sweet regional specialty that's perfect on both hot summer and mild winter days. Out in the orchard, you'll see how dates cluster and grow as you enjoy a few minutes in the shade of the thickly fronded palm trees.

Another famous date orchard that's open to the public is the **Shields Date Farm** (80–225 Hwy. 111, Indio, 800/414-2555, www.shields dates.com, daily 9 A.M.–5 P.M.) in Indio. If you can't make it as far as Oasis, check it out!

Desert Memorial Park
It's not on most tourist destination lists for Palm Springs, but visiting star seekers and locals alike make pilgrimages to Desert Memorial Park (31750 Da Vall Dr., Cathedral City). Unlike the craggy old cemeteries in more historically oriented parts of California, you won't find slightly sunken marble tombstones, illegible wooden board memorials, or dried up weeds. Here all the grave markers are flat and uniform, the deep green lawn is meticulously maintained, and the shade trees are trimmed to perfection. Stop by the office to pick up a map and listing of the graves, some of which are inhabited by the remains of famous Hollywood celebrities. The best known of these are Frank Sinatra and Sonny Bono. Several members of Sinatra's family rest beside him. You might also see the markers for members of the Gabor family and actor William Powell.

ENTERTAINMENT AND EVENTS
Unlike most of the rest of California's desert towns, Palm Springs is a thriving entertainment center. If you love to see shows, go out dancing, and stay up till 3 A.M. partying, this is the town

© LANCE SCOTT

Oasis Date Farm

for you! The nightlife has a friendly vibe, the shows appeal to all ages (for real), and the festivals can fill the whole town with fun-loving visitors from around California and beyond.

Bars and Clubs

Red 74 (72–990 El Paseo, Palm Desert, 760/568-6774, Tues.–Sat. 6 P.M.–2 A.M., cover $5–15) in the suburb of Palm Desert offers truth in advertising; red fabric adorns the walls, and red decorative elements create a womblike monochromatic atmosphere. You'll find a younger crowd here enjoying the original signature cocktails, the dancing, and the eye candy. Beware: You might find yourself trying to grab a drink during a six-minute speed-dating session. But if you're lucky, you'll make it on a night with world music or a particularly good local DJ.

Two other suburban bar/clubs you can try out are the **Village Lounge** (73196 Hwy. 111, Palm Desert, 760/568-1200) and the **Club Rio** (68449 Perez Rd., Cathedral City, 760/321-5526).

Gay and Lesbian

To be frank, most of the good nightlife in Palm Springs sits squarely within the gay community. The liveliest bars, the best dance clubs, the smoothest lounges—all gay.

But then again, "gay bar" doesn't mean quite the same thing in Palm Springs as it does in San Francisco or even Los Angeles. Here in the desert, there's a very casual, relaxed vibe to almost all of these spots. There's far less regimentation of straight vs. gay vs. lesbian here than elsewhere in California. It's not at all unusual to hit a gay bar at 11 P.M. on a Saturday night and find pretty shirtless boys, crew-cut lesbians, gorgeous drag queens, threesomes of indeterminate relationship, and straight married senior citizens all grooving on the same dance floor. Most "gay" bars and clubs welcome straights of all ages—just be aware that you'll see open same-sex affection, and if you freak out over it, *you'll* be the one who's asked to leave. Same goes the other way; if you're gay, you're expected to tolerate straight folks smooching on your turf. But if you're open minded about your fun, you'll love the scene here in Palm Springs.

One of the premier gay clubs in Palm Springs offers you a respite from the desert heat at the **Oasis Nightclub & Lounge** (611 S. Palm Canyon Dr., 760/416-0950, www.cluboasis ps.com, Wed.–Thurs. 3 P.M.–midnight, Fri. until 2 A.M., Sat. until 4 A.M.). The regrettable strip-mall exterior belies the big industrial interior, which includes tons of room for dancing as well as drinking and meeting people. The unfinished ceiling and ductwork make the dance floor feel bigger, anyway. The crowd tends towards the boys, but women are welcome too. The club hosts many parties and special events each year, plus a regular calendar of nightly fun. Go to the website for more information before you come, or just show up and be surprised. Looking for a slightly mellower evening? Order your favorite fruity cocktail at the **O Lounge,** a quieter spot within the Oasis.

If your tastes run to leather, the one club in Palm Springs you must visit is **The Tool Shed** (600 E. Sunny Dunes Rd., 760/320-3299, www.toolshed-ps.com, daily 7 A.M.–2 A.M., Fri.–Sat. until 3 A.M.). Wear your leather and your Levi's when you come to shoot a game of pool or enjoy the rugged scenery. Inside, you'll find mostly men drinking and having fun in the appropriately industrial-styled bar, complete with chain-link fence. Check the website for a list of upcoming events.

For the ladies, **Delilah's** (67855 Hwy. 111, Cathedral City, 760/770-1210) offers a more estrogen-oriented atmosphere.

A newcomer on the proverbial block, **Mixie's Boy Bar** (120 S. Palm Canyon Dr., 760/203-0147) offers a big, meandering, multi-level dance floor, two bars, and a patio where you can hang out and smoke. The video system provides nonstop visual entertainment (as if the dance floor wasn't enough!) and DJ Mixtress rocks the house with a totally danceable blend of hip-hop, house, pop, and the occasional '80s classic thrown in to keep things lively. The art prints on the wall definitely have a theme, and there's actually a fair amount of seating for patrons who aren't quite up to dancing the whole night away. Is that totally shapely cocktail waitress male or female? Does it matter? This club and bar is one of the all-sexualities-welcome establishments, so feel free to climb the stairs for a fun late-night party no matter what your proclivities.

Even in gala Palm Springs, **Toucan's Tiki Lounge** (2100 N. Palm Canyon Dr., 760/416-7584, www.toucanstikilounge.com) draws notice. It's also a locals' favorite, almost a bar-around-the-corner, despite the wild tiki decor. This fun nightspot has pretty boy go-go dancers, a tiny dance floor that gets crowded on weekends, and a drag show every Sunday night. Bring a friend or four to make the most of a night out at Toucan's.

Can you picture a gay sports bar? **Score** (301 E. Arenas Rd., 760/866-1905) brings these two usually mutually exclusive concepts together to create a unique queer-jock experience on Arena Road, the longtime gay main drag. Imagine big-screen TVs, beer on tap, and dozens of beautiful men to stare at. Sounds like heaven!

Live Shows

One of the staples of the Palm Springs entertainment scene is its exuberant Vegas-style shows. With singing, dancing, amazing costumes, and wonderful comedy, these shows delight audiences all year long.

Perhaps the most popular of the big shows is the **Palm Springs Follies** (128 S. Palm Canyon Dr., 760/327-0225, www.psfollies.com, shows Wed.–Sun. most weeks, see current schedule, $48–90). This vaudeville-meets-Vegas-style show draws national guest acts (Oct.–May). So what's the twist? Those lovely bejeweled showgirls wearing the glitter and the giant feather headdresses are old. Really, really old. The youngest performer in the Palm Springs Follies is 54 years old, and the oldest showgirl is well past her 80th birthday. You'll be surprised and delighted by a cast that's old enough to remember when this kind of live singing and dancing entertainment was more

than just a curiosity. Heck, a few of these performers remember Prohibition! Perhaps best of all, the dancers and singers come out to meet their audience after each show. Get autographs on your program and express your appreciation of the sexy seniors.

Advance reservations are highly recommended, as the Palm Springs Follies often sells out. You can purchase tickets for this three-hour show online or by phone, or at the box office. This long show can get boring quickly for small children, so it might be better to leave them at home, especially for evening shows.

Visitors who want to blend the various cultures of Palm Springs can't help but love **Copy Katz** (Casino Morongo Resort and Spa, 49500 Seminole Dr., Cabazon, 800/252-4499, www.morongocasinoresort.com or www.copykatzps.com). This celebrity impersonator and drag show features talented performers who'll make you believe you're watching Barbra Streisand or Michael Jackson. You can check online for the shows coming up in the following week, and you can buy tickets at the website. Cabazon is 20 minutes west of Palm Springs.

Festivals and Events

With tourism and glamour as its major industries, it's no surprise that the Palm Springs area hosts an immense array of festivals each year to bring even more visitors into town.

One of the biggest festivals each year celebrates the area's signature crop: dates. The **Riverside County Fair and Date Festival** (82–503 Hwy. 111, Indio, 760/863-8247, www.datefest.org, Mon.–Fri. 10 A.M.–10 P.M., Sat.–Sun. 10 A.M.–midnight, adults $8, youth 5–12 $6) takes place in mild and lovely February of each year at the County Fairground in Indio. The Fairgrounds were created with a fun and funky Arabian Nights theme, which decorates the big space from the entrance gates inward. Be sure to get a place to view the Queen Scheherazade parade, check out the ostrich and camel races, and definitely grab a date shake from one of the many vendors. Kids and teens flock to the carnival area to ride the tilting, whirling, zipping rides (unlimited rides $23) that light up at night. You can't help but be entertained as you ramble through the rows of vendors, view the county fair contest entrants, and taste every dish that can possibly be made with dates. In the evenings, musical acts draw fairgoers to the stage to watch everything from local jazz to headlining national classic rock acts.

A perennial favorite of serious rock lovers from all over the state is the **Coachella Valley Music Festival** (www.coachella.com, single-day pass $95, three-day pass $275). Literally dozens of bands crowd onto the roster each year. In 2008, the lineup featured Roger Waters as the headliner, with such bands as The Verve, Death Cab for Cutie, and Fatboy Slim adding spice. For three days, concertgoers can immerse themselves in music from sunup to sundown and beyond. (Well, not quite from sunup...your hangover will appreciate the restraint.)

The Festival runs over a long weekend each spring, usually toward the end of April. Attendees can choose from the endless array of local motels and inns, or they can bring tents to pitch on-site so as to stick as close as possible to the action. The festival is held at the Empire Polo Field. Car access isn't too difficult, but the festival organizers encourage the use of public transit and carpooling to minimize auto traffic and crowding in the parking lots. Check the website for gate-opening hours and current prices. You can buy tickets online through the festival site, or call one of the major ticket handlers.

To no one's surprise, the Palm Springs region holds not one but many gay-themed events each year. While the annual **Greater Palm Springs Pride Parade** (www.pspride.org, Nov.) and festival are plenty of fun and well-attended, and the **Dinah Shore Weekend** (www.dinah shoreweekend.com, Apr.) is held especially for the girls, these are not *the* events of the season. Instead, break out your best croquet whites and take yourself and your friends to the annual **White Party** (277 Avenida Caballeros, www .jeffreysanker.com). Although the signature party takes place on the third Saturday night

of April each year, the whole week beforehand sees pool parties, after-hours club events, and plenty of other themed social entertainments livening up the nights. The Saturday night White Party hosts up to 20,000 white-clad men intent on bumping and grinding and dancing the night away to fabulous, top-end DJs. Drag and dance shows light up the stage throughout the evening, and side lounges offer spots to sit down, kick back, and relax...or while away...in a quieter space. The White Party typically runs 9 P.M.–5 A.M., with an after-party for seriously dedicated partiers. Other festival-sponsored parties include the fabulous and very popular Underwear Party and Pool Party. Check the website to buy tickets for your favorite events and get a look at this year's theme.

SHOPPING

Shopping is a major pastime for the wealthy golfers and condo owners who frequent the Palm Springs area. The whole of Palm Canyon Drive from La Quinta up to Palm Springs seems to be one long strip mall, with everything from auto parts shops to Targets and on up through high-end chain clothing stores. On the other hand, for unique boutiques, your best bet is downtown Palm Springs or El Paseo.

El Paseo

El Paseo is actually a mile-long avenue in the town of Palm Desert. Literally hundreds of shops, galleries, salons, restaurants, and more cluster on both sides of this legendary shopping street. El Paseo hosts a number of festivals each year, and weekly Art Walks during the wintertime high season. Whether you've come for the culture or for some simple retail therapy, El Paseo can hook you up.

The largest block of shops, an outdoor mall of sorts, is called **The Gardens** (El Paseo and San Pablo). The Gardens is anchored by Saks Fifth Avenue (73–555 El Paseo, 760/837-2900, www.saksfifthavenue.com, Mon.–Thurs. 10 A.M.–6 P.M., Fri.–Sat. 10 A.M.–7 P.M., Sun. 11 A.M.–6 P.M.) on one side and Tiffany & Co. (73–585 El Paseo, 760/341-3444, www .tiffany.com, Mon.–Sat. 10 A.M.–6 P.M., Sun.

11 A.M.–5 P.M.) on the other. But you can walk, or take one of the bright-yellow Courtesy Carts from end to end of the long street to make carrying your accumulation of shopping bags a bit easier.

At the south end, between Ocotillo and Sage Streets, shoppers interested in Native Americana and New Age merchandise can find an array of lovely things at shops such as **Earth Spirits** (73–130 El Paseo #N., 760/779-8766). Apparel for men and women can be purchased all up and down El Paseo—choose from chain shops or unique boutiques such as **She She** (73–061 El Paseo, Ste. 2, 760/779-0417) and **Mister Marcus** (73–540 El Paseo, Ste. B, 776-8454). Art lovers enjoy wandering in the **Edenhurst Gallery** (73–655 El Paseo, 760/346-7900) and **Gallery 1000** (73–400 El Paseo, #1, 760/346-2230), among others. The street also hosts an endless selection of interior designers and home stores for those looking to pick up just the right Southwestern item to add to their home's decor.

Outlets

Outside of Palm Springs, you can load up on discount designer merchandise at the **Desert Hills Premium Outlets** (48400 Seminole Dr., Cabazon, 951/849-6641, http://premiumoutlets.com/deserthills, Sun.–Thurs. 10 A.M.–8 P.M., Fri. 10 A.M.–9 P.M., Sat. 9 A.M.–9 P.M.). From Palm Springs, drive west on Highway 11 to I-10 and into Cabazon. Highlights of this huge sprawl of high-end outlet stores include Dolce & Gabbana, Ralph Lauren, Gucci, Cole Haan, Waterford Wedgewood, and Bose. If all that bargain-hunting makes you hungry or you need a hit of energy, the mall has an array of coffee shops and quickie restaurants at each end to satisfy your cravings.

SPORTS AND RECREATION

The Palm Springs and Coachella Valley area hosts a staggering 100-plus golf courses. If you're not a golf lover, beautiful desert and mountain parks beckon hikers and even cross-country skiers and showshoers. Water parks cool children and adults alike during the long, hot desert summers.

Parks

The closest gorgeous scenery and good hiking to downtown Palm Springs is found at the **Indian Canyons** (1097 E. Murray Canyon Rd., 760/327-6550, www.palmsprings.com/points/canyon, daily 8 A.M.–5 P.M., adults $8, children $4). These canyons were once home to the ancestors of the Agua Caliente Cahuilla Native Americans. The abundant streams and diverse plant and animal species made the series of canyons a wonderful place to live—plenty of fresh drinking water, food, and materials to build shelter sit all around. The progressive tribes even diverted water from the streams to irrigate planted crops. Today, all the canyons bear trace evidence of these long-gone communities, and it's fun for kids (and grown-ups) to search for housing foundations, dam remnants, and food-processing areas.

The most stunning (and most-visited) of the canyons is **Palm Canyon,** an aptly named 15-mile-long oasis of color, water, and beauty improbably set in the midst of a dry and barren patch of desert. You'll bask in the shade of the lush and naturally growing palm trees, admire the colorful spring wildflowers, and dip your fingers in the creek that feeds the abundant life in the canyon. The paved footpath makes it easy to explore. For an extra $3, you can take a ranger-guided one-mile walk to learn more about the history and nature of the canyon. Or if you prefer to let a strong equine do the walking, horseback riding is permitted through Palm Canyon. And in the grand tradition of popular outdoor sights in Southern California, the **Trading Post** offers souvenirs, maps, and refreshments to all comers.

Another beautiful and well-traveled spot is **Tahquitz Canyon** (500 W. Mesquite Rd., 760/416-7044, adults $12.50, children $6). The highlight of Tahquitz Canyon is a waterfall that cascades down 60 feet down and splashes into a pool. The fall is seasonal, and you'll want to come in the springtime to see the best show. Tahquitz Canyon has its own

© LIZ HAMILL SCOTT

Snow in Palm Springs!

visitors center, complete with an interpretive exhibit, short educational film, and observation deck.

Other canyons include **Murray Canyon** and **Andreas Canyon.** If you prefer seclusion and a wilder version of natural beauty, these canyons might be more appealing to you than the well-developed Tahquitz and Palm Canyons.

At the top of the Aerial Tramway, **Mount San Jacinto State Park** (25905 Hwy. 243, 951/659-2607, www.parks.ca.gov, daily dawn–dusk) offers fabulous hiking, camping, and winter snow play only 10 minutes from Palm Springs by gondola ride. You can also access the park from the other side by driving in from CA-243 or CA-74. The south end of the Pacific Crest Trail runs through this beautiful high-elevation park. Many day-hike trails crisscross the mountain peak, letting visitors enjoy cool, shaded forests and fabulous valley views as they walk. A number of campgrounds throughout the park, some hike-in and some car-campsites, offer outdoorsy travelers the opportunity to acclimate to the altitude and explore the area in depth. But no matter how fit you are, take care when you first arrive and begin to hike here—you'll be well over a mile and possibly as much as two miles above sea level, and altitude sickness can be a real danger.

Nature lovers can look for lots of wildlife as they ply the trails of the park. Sniff the wildflowers and admire the butterflies drinking from them, touch the bark of a Jeffrey Pine tree, or bring your birding list and look out for winged friends. While bears aren't a problem at San Jacinto, do keep an eye out for mountain lions. If you see one, get as big as you can and don't run; face the cat down.

Golf

The major form of outdoor exercise in and around Palm Springs and the Coachella Valley is golf. The region boasts more than 100 courses, about half of which are public or semi-public. The rest belong to a variety of private country clubs. Among the publicly accessible courses, players can try anything from low-fee municipal courses up to swanky PGA championship country clubs. If you're a serious golfer, pick up a guide to all the courses or look on the web to find those that will fit your game best.

Indian Springs Golf and Country Club (79-940 Westward Ho Dr., Indio, 760/200-8988, www.indianspringsgc.com) boasts some of the best golfing in all the region for under $100 (most of the time). Naturally, the best rates going are in the blistering summertime, but you can find bargains in the moderate months of September, October, and March as well. Whatever your skill level, this 6,770-yard, par 72 course will offer fun in the desert sunshine. You can also make good use of the driving range and pro shop, and grab breakfast, lunch, or dinner before or after your game.

Looking for hardcore championship golf the likes of which you've only seen before on TV? Book a tee time at **Trilogy La Quinta** (60–151 Trilogy Pkwy., La Quinta, 760/771-0707, www .trilogygolfclub.com/laquinta, $30–120). The likes of Tiger Woods and Annika Sorenstam have walked the greens here at the oftentimes home of the PGA Skins Game. Six tee positions provide a challenge for new, mid-level, and experienced players. As at most courses, afternoon golfers get the best price breaks, as do those willing to brave the torturous summer heat. The attached Azul Restaurant has gone modern in its decor, serving upscale California cuisine for breakfast, lunch, and dinner to golfers and non-players alike.

The **Cimarron Golf Resort** (67–603 30th Ave., Cathedral City, 760/777-6060, www .cimarrongolf.com) prides itself on offering a different experience from the plethora of country club courses. In truth it has two separate courses: Pebble and Boulder. Boulder is the par-71 championship course that draws the best golfers out on weekend morning, while Pebble's par-58 provides fun for even the newest of golfers and good practice for more advanced players who only have a couple of hours to enjoy a game. You can book your tee time up to 120 days in advance. Call for rates during your stay.

SAFETY IN THE DESERT

People who've never spent time in a desert before often underestimate the very real dangers of trekking in a harsh, dry climate, while experienced desert rats can become overconfident and complacent about their safety precautions, to their detriment.

No matter who you are, or how many times you've gone hiking or camping or backpacking or driving out into the desert, you *must* plan for problems and practice for safety. Here are a few recommendations from the various desert state and national parks:

- **Carry water.** This is possibly *the* most important desert safety tip of them all. You're not likely to find much water if you're out hiking in the desert. In Death Valley, 1-2 gallon per person per day is recommended, and they mean it. Even if you're driving around the park on mostly paved roads, carry water in your car. Water is a big concern in all the big desert parks – you won't find much, even at the major sights with big parking

lots. No matter which desert you're visiting or for how long, bring twice as much water as you think you'll need. Better to have too much than too little!

- **Wear a hat.** In the desert, wear a hat with a wide brim to shade your face and your neck. Do it even if you hate hats; if you don't have one, buy one at the gift shop. Hats are the single best way to keep the punishing desert sun off your head, a must if you get into any trouble in the desert.

- **Wear sunglasses.** Again, don shades even if they're not your usual style. The harsh sunlight bouncing off the light-colored landscape can cause real damage to unprotected eyes. Many of the visitors centers sell sunglasses.

- **Use sunscreen.** You've never experienced sun like it pounds down in the desert, so be good to your skin and go for a high-SPF sun-

Looking for something else? A few more of seemingly infinite options include **Eagle Falls Golf Course** (84–245 Indio Springs Parkway, Indio, 760/238-5633, www.eaglefallsgolf.com, $50), **Mesquite** (2700 E. Mesquite Ave., Palm Springs, 800/727-8331, www.palmsprings.com/golf/mesquite.html), where Bob Hope used to bring his cronies, and the ritzy **Indian Wells Golf Resort** (44-500 Indian Wells Ln., Indian Wells, 760/346-4653, www.indianwellsgolfresort.com, $75–200).

Biking

Bicycling opportunities abound in Palm Springs. Wintertime, when the weather is mild to cool, is the best time to take a bike out on the desert roads and bike trails. In the city of Palm Springs, an interconnected maze of bike trails help folks get around with ease and relative safety. Check www.palmsprings.com/city/palmsprings/bikemap.html for a map of the in-town loops.

Water Parks

Summer visitors and locals looking to both cool off and enjoy active outdoor fun head for **Knott's Soak City USA** (1500 S. Gene Autry Tr., 760/327-0499, www.knotts.com/soakcity/ps/index.shtml, adults $18–30, children $18). As with most major California water parks, Soak City has fast and furious slides, as well as the funky new Pacific Spin, a slow-moving river for inner tubers, a wave pool, and a children's splash area. Soak City also offers plenty of dry land, complete with some chairs and chaises. Amenities include coin-op lockers, food concessions, restrooms and changing rooms, and rentable shaded cabanas.

Winter Sports

With the well-known scorching desert climate of the valley floor, Palm Springs doesn't seem like much of a winter sports destination. And yet, visitors and locals (especially locals) can take advantage of nearby mountains to ski,

---

screen. (It'll also help with the unbelievably dry skin most folks get when hanging out in ultra-dry climates.)

- **Stay away from old mines and other man-made hazards.** You'll find cool old abandoned mines in Death Valley, Joshua Tree, Mojave, and possibly even Anza-Borrego. Such places have zillions of hidden dangers, from invisible vertical shafts to collapsing timbers to piles of old explosives. Don't wander into old mine shafts or touch explosives, and tell park rangers about the latter.

- **Be aware of potential flash floods.** All the desert parks in California are rife with washes – spots where water rushes across the landscape during rare but often intense desert storms. And if you're in a wash during one of those storms, you can get fatally swept away. If the weather looks stormy, take care in washes: don't park your car

in one, don't use one for a hiking trail, and don't pitch your tent in or beside a wash.

- **Tell someone where you're going.** Tell a friend or a family member back home where you're going and when you plan to be home. That way, somebody will miss you if you don't come back and can alert the park or the police to your potential location and predicament. If you're planning to go backcountry camping in a park that allows it, register with the rangers as required for the same reason.

- **If something happens, stick with your vehicle or your companions.** It's easier to find several people than one alone, and it's easier to find a bright shiny car than it is a person. So if the worst happens and you find yourself stranded, stay with your group and with your car for the best chance of being found.

sled, snowboard, or just play in the snow for a day.

For a nearby day of snow play, cross-country skiing, or snowshoeing, grab your gear and take the Palm Springs Aerial Tramway up to **Mount San Jacinto State Park** (25905 Hwy. 243, 951/659-2607, www.parks.ca.gov, daily dawn–dusk). If you've got sleds and kids, head out of the Mountain Station and down the main trail to the Adventure Center. Here you'll find groomed sledding tracks and even the occasional sled-racing event. For the adventurous and fit crowd, many of the summer hiking trails turn into cross-country ski and snowshoe tracks when the snow covers them. Check with the rangers at the Mountain Station for current conditions and a trail map.

SoCal downhill skiers and snowboarders think of the ski resorts at **Big Bear** (880 Summit Blvd., 800/424-4232, http://bigbear.com) as their home mountains. Choose between **Snow Summit** (909/866-5766, www.snowsummit.com, adult lift tickets $20–65, children $8–53) and **Bear Mountain** (909/866-5766, www.bearmountain.com). At Snow Summit, 14 lifts service more than 30 trails. This resort caters primarily to beginning and intermediate skiers, complete with a ski school and fun beginner terrain parks. On the other hand, Bear Mountain appeals more to the intermediate and advanced crowd. With dozens of jumps, jibs, and a Superpipe, Bear Mountain beckons to boarders and freestylers from SoCal and beyond.

Big Bear also offers cross-country ski and snowshoeing trails and tours, plus a snow park.

Spas

With all that money running around Palm Springs, it's understandable that plenty of it gets spent on relaxing massages and rejuvenating facials. You'll find many day spas and spa resorts clustered north of Palm Springs proper in the town of Desert Hot Springs, taking advantage of the smallish locale's namesake waters. For example, **Living Waters Spa** (13340 Mountain View Rd., Desert Hot Springs,

866/329-9988, www.livingwatersspa.com, day use $45/couple or single) features multiple pools filled with the local mineral water, massage services, and comfortable European-style hotel accommodations (most with full kitchens). The other European aspect of Living Waters its clothing-optional and, in fact, somewhat clothing-discouraged facilities. Expect to see day-use and overnight guests strolling, bathing, and lounging in the nude all around the resort. The emphasis of this spa is on freedom (especially freedom from binding clothing) and relaxation for all visitors.

On the other hand, **Desert Mystique Spa** (4721 E. Palm Canyon Dr., Ste. F, Palm Springs, 760/960-4597, www.desertmystiquespa.com, Mon.–Sat. 10 A.M.–7 P.M., Sun. by appt, $80–90/hour massage) in the midst of downtown Palm Springs gives more modest spa-goers a traditional day spa experience. Desert Mystique has a full menu of spa treatments, including half a dozen different massage styles and an array of facial and body treatments. The facials tend toward SoCal aesthetic and post-surgical treatments, while the massages have an almost Northern California flair.

If you're serious about pampering your face, book an appointment at **European Experience Luxury Facials** (2225 Tahquitz Canyon Rd., Ste. 6, Palm Springs, 760/902-2751, www.palmspringsfacials.com). Whether you're a man or a woman, this day spa can concoct the perfect treatment. Men also seek out the specialized back treatment, and everyone loves a relaxing Swedish massage. Ear candling and waxing services are also available.

Casino Gambling

The **Fantasy Springs Casino** (84-245 Indian Springs Pkwy, Indio, 800/827-2946, www.fantasyspringsresort.com) has all sorts of entertainment options, from bowling to live shows. You can stay at the high-rise hotel and pass all day and half the night down on the casino floor. This isn't a full-fledged Vegas-style casino, but you'll find plenty of slot machines, table games, bingo, and even horse-race betting. Enjoy a game of easy-rules blackjack or mini-baccarat, or try your luck at one of the newer progressive slot machines. When you need a break, head for one of several restaurants or the nearby attached cocktail bar.

At the **Spa Resort Casino** (401 E. Amado Rd., Palm Springs, 760/883-1000, www.spa resortcasino.com) you can try your luck at one of 1,000 slot machines or 30 tables. Got lots of cash to bet? Head for the high-limit room. Poker lovers tend to stick close to the card room, while casual gamers take a break from the endless noises and flashing lights of the casino floor to get a soothing massage or facial at the resort's in-house spa.

ACCOMMODATIONS

The range of accommodations in Palm Springs is both broad and deep. As a town with nearly 100 years' history as a tourist mecca, it's hard not to find a room here, even on the spur of the moment (as long as it's not a festival weekend). You can go for a cheap motel, a historic mid-century modern hotel with Hollywood history, or even a plush high-end casino style hotel. Sure, you can stay at one of the standard national chain motels, but why would you when so many lovely boutique hotels dot the landscape?

If you're gay, you've got even more choices. Palm Springs has an array of gay-only and gay-friendly lodgings. Most of these cater to men only, except during the woman-oriented Dinah Shore Weekend.

Under $100

Chase Hotel Palm Springs (200 W. Arenas Rd., 760/320-8866, www.chasehotelpalm springs.com, $90–235) offers classic Palm Springs–style accommodations at reasonable nightly or weekly rates. The charming mid-century modern motel sits only a block from Palm Canyon Drive. Outdoors, it boasts a charming garden area complete with palm trees and a saline swimming pool. Inside, while the style of the guest room furnishings evokes the 1950s, the beds and chair are in fact comfortable and totally modern. Choose between a king or two-bed room, or a larger suite with

a kitchenette and perhaps even a mosaic-tiled fireplace. Each morning, grab a bite to eat from the tasty continental breakfast spread, and don't forget to indulge in a freshly baked chocolate chip cookie in the evening!

$100-150

Only a few minutes from the center of town, **◖ A Place in the Sun** (754 E. San Lorenzo Rd., 760/325-0254, www.aplaceinthesun hotel.com, $112–340) was first built in the early 1950s to shelter the cast and crew working on the film of the same name. Then and now, a meandering set of 16 semi-individual bungalows offer spacious quarters for visitors. All guest bungalows include full kitchens, living rooms with modern TVs, and tropical-resort-style decor with old-school movie prints decorating the rather thin walls. Bedrooms have cushy mattresses and older wall heaters—you might even see a radiator unit original to the property in your vintage pink-tiled bathroom. You'll also have your own small private patio (on which you can relax with a cigarette),

© LANCE SCOTT

A Place in the Sun

plus access to the central courtyard with its ill-kept miniature putting green and its lovely modern gentle-salt pool and spa. A continental breakfast is served in the office each day, or out in the gazebo by the pool with more variety of food and drink on the weekends in wintertime. Friendly owners will help you out with all aspects of your stay (the office is open 9 A.M.–5 P.M. six days per week). Pets are welcome.

If you want to stay in a real William F. Cody original building, check in to the **Del Marcos Hotel** (225 W. Baristo Rd., 760/325-6902, www.delmarcoshotel.com, $110–200). This small boutique hotel has won awards for its dedication to preserving its mid-century modern design. Indeed, even the guest room decor screams late 1940s and early '50s, complete with prints of Hollywood idols of the time, period artwork, and brightly colored chairs of funky design. You'll be greeted at the front entrance by the hallmark diagonally sloping roofs and faux-stonework, and muted colors of the period. The interior courtyard boasts a saline pool surrounded by chaise lounges with umbrellas and an expanse of concrete. With only 16 rooms, the Del Marcos Hotel feels more like an inn than an impersonal hotel, and it's convenient to the shops and restaurants of Palm Canyon Drive.

$150-250

The **Movie Colony Hotel** (726 N. Indian Canyon Dr., 888/953-5700, www.movie colonyhotel.com, $180–400) takes the famed mid-century modern style and kicks it into an upper scale. While you'll still see the clean diagonal lines and blocky structural details, the amenities inside and out of the rooms and townhouses here breathe with a vintage-meets-modern luxury. You'll find high thread-count linens, light-colored designer furnishings, plenty of space, and designer accents. All rooms have California king beds and pristine bathrooms. Townhouses include large living areas with great 1950s style sofas, fireplaces, and travertine bars with refrigerators. Pay a little extra for a room with a door out to the attractive pool area. It's the focal point of the

hotel, and includes a large spa and a fire pit where complimentary wine is served in the evenings. With your room rate, you'll also receive a daily continental breakfast, concierge service, and loaner bicycles on which you can explore downtown Palm Springs.

Over $250

If you can afford serious luxury in the desert, stay at the **Villa Royale Inn** (1620 S. Indian Trail, 760/327-2314, www.villaroyale.com, $200–350). This lovely boutique hotel seeks to evoke the feel of Europe—a Tuscan villa, perhaps. Guest rooms range from small "hideaways" to spacious two-bedroom villas that feel more like home than a hotel room. Each of the 30 rooms has its own unique antique furnishings, down duvet, fluffy bathrobes, and charming bathroom stocked with herbal toiletries. Though the rooms are fabulous, it's the amenities at Villa Royale that make you feel like royalty. Choose between two pools and one large Jacuzzi, book an in-room massage, or ask the concierge to help you get a tee time or a tennis court at one of the famed local golf courses or country clubs. Every morning you'll awaken to a full, hot, cooked-to-order breakfast, which can be served in your room. For lunch and dinner, enjoy the Continental cuisine served by the attached restaurant Europa, or have them bring the food to you in your room or out at poolside.

Gay and Lesbian Resorts

Among the dozens of resort hotels and inns catering to gay men, **The Triangle Inn** (555 E. San Lorenzo Rd., 760/322-7993, www.pride nation.com/triangle, $135–560) stands out for a number of reasons. The Triangle was the first commercial design of one Hugh Kaptur, the architect who went on to do much important mid-century modern work in and around Palm Springs, including William Holden's home. The unique structures and interesting lines have been preserved, making the lushly landscaped buildings fun to look at for passersby outside the compound. Inside, each of the nine guest suites has a unique decorative scheme.

le of days in advance, since Wang's gets
ded with locals at dinnertime, especially
eekends.

nch

en you turn sideways to thread your way
Pomme Frite (256 S. Palm Canyon
, 760/778-3727, www.pomme-frite.com,
ch Sat.–Sun. 11:30 A.M.–2:30 P.M., dinner
d.–Mon. 4:30–10:30 P.M., $18–28), you
ght believe you've somehow been transported
France or even Belgium. This hole-in-the-
ll does not pretend to serve haute cuisine; in-
ad, Pomme Frite offers casual bistro dishes
oked to perfection. The food fits in perfectly
th the atmosphere—sunny yellow walls,
ack-and-white prints, real wooden wine boxes,
d other tchotchkes. Tables are scrunched so
ose together in the tiny front dining room that
ven the wait staff has trouble getting through.
hough the back dining room's setup is a
iny bit more spacious, it's still loud and has a
riendly, crowded feeling. On weekends, reser-
ations are highly recommended, though they
fit in as many walk-ins as they can.

The menu provides a look at both Paris bras-
serie favorites such as mussels and steak and
fries, plus a few fun Belgian dishes. The fresh,
delicate salads are delicious too, but as you eat,
try to save just a little bit of room for the delectable desserts.

Italian

Do you just want an ultra-casual pizza meal?
Walk up to the counter at **Lotza Mozza
Pizza & Pasta** (119 S. Indian Canyon Dr.,
760/325-5571, $10) and order a handmade
pizza, a tasty pasta dish, or a big crisp salad.
Grab a seat at any of the red-checker-covered
tables and the cute young wait staff will bring
your food out to you. Pizzas have New York–
style thin crusts, tasty tomato sauce, and gooey
mozzarella cheese. While the service isn't always stellar, the price is right and the food does
come out piping hot and tasty.

Mexican

Among the best of the many Mexican

restaurants throughout the Palm Springs
region, the **Las Casuela** (368 N. Palm
Canyon Dr., 760/325-3213, www.lascasuelas
.com, Sun.–Thurs. 11 A.M.–9 P.M., Fri.–Sat.
11 A.M.–9:30 P.M., $10–12) group offers some
of the best and most authentic Mexican cuisine. Las Casuela Original was the first of
them, opened by the Delgado family in 1958
with the recipes Maria brought up from her
home. The small dining room looks bigger because of the wall-length mirror along one side,
which reflects the wonderful hand-painted
mural on the opposite walls that depicts pas-
toral life in Mexico, complete with cows.
The service feels as friendly as the restaurant
sounds—if you have any food allergies or special requests, they'll be happy to accommodate
you. The family opened Las Casuela Nuevas
and **Las Casuela Terraza** (222 S. Palm
Canyon Dr.), two bigger and slightly fancier
versions of the original, still using Grandma's
old recipes as the basis for their menus. Terraza
boasts a beautiful outdoor patio seating area
and some fabulous margaritas made with top-
shelf tequilas.

Steak

The restaurateurs of Palm Springs have opened
a near-countless array of steakhouses. It's hard
to go more than a mile or two without running into one. The king of the local chains is
undoubtedly **LG's Prime Steakhouse** (255 S.
Palm Canyon Dr., Ste. B, 760/416-1779, www
.lgsprimesteakhouse.com, daily 5 P.M.–close,
$25–55). All three of their restaurants (one in
Palm Springs, one in Palm Desert, and one in
La Quinta) offer the best beef available, much
of it dry aged in specially designed meat lockers
on the premises. The sides are steakhouse clas-
sics that complement the huge cuts of meat, but
some of the appetizers are LG's originals. While
the atmosphere at LG's has a splash of upscale
elegance, you'll still see plenty of exposed brick
and feel a touch of casual friendliness.

Vegetarian

Desperately looking for a meat-free meal in
steak-loving Palm Springs? Head downtown

You can rent anything from a studio suite up to a fully furnished four-bedroom house. Out at the pool, in the hot tub, under the cooling misters, and in the other common areas of the Triangle, clothing is optional. Hosts Michael and Stephen live at the resort and their talent as hosts helps make the Triangle what it is today. Oh, and be sure to pet Duncan, the orange tabby cat who runs the place, when you see him prowling the grounds.

A larger oasis for gay men, the **Vista Grande Resorts** (574 S. Warm Sands Dr., 760/322-2404, www.mirage4men.com, $100–325) sits in the popular Warm Sands area. This hedonistic clothing-optional resort offers 30-some guest rooms, three pools, three spas, and a steam room. The pool-and-spa complex in the Mirage section of the three-resort complex has two waterfalls, curved naturalistic pools, and lots of foliage and rocks surrounding the swimmable waters. Rooms range from an economical studio room to a luxurious suite by the waterfall with a living room and a full kitchen. All amenities are taken care of, so kick back, relax by (or in) the pool, and concentrate on making new friends.

For the ladies, the **Queen of Hearts** (435 E. Avenida Olancha, 760/322-5793, www .queenofheartsps.com, $120–180) provides laid-back elegance for reasonable nightly rates. This recently renovated nine-room inn was the first lesbian-oriented hotel to be opened in Palm Springs nearly 40 years ago (then called the Desert Knight). Today, each room includes lovely light designer appointments, a queen bed, a full kitchen, and a comfortable bathroom. Unlike the men's resorts, guests of the Queen of Hearts wear clothes in the common areas, including while swimming in the sparkling courtyard pool or soaking in the outdoor, above-ground whirlpool tub. While you don't need to be a gay woman or couple to stay at the Queen, this inn does cater to that crowd and you should expect to see happy female couples engaging in public displays of affection here. If you're among those couples, be sure to let management know if you're celebrating a birthday or anniversary!

FOOD

The dining in Palm Springs exe~~i~~ of California. You'll find high- and French cuisine, fun ethni~~c~~ tasty snack foods all through th~~e~~ the greatest concentration of ser~~.~~ dent restaurants collects downt~~own~~ around Palm Canyon Drive.

American

A favorite local downtown break~~fast~~ **Billy Reed's** (1800 N. Palm C~~a~~ 760/325-1946, daily 7 A.M.–9 P.M~~.~~ The interior dining room and ba~~r~~ lights and air conditioning, while th~~e~~ patio offers plenty of seating and gre~~at~~ watching. The casual atmosphere ~~welcomes~~ everyone all day long, though shoes a~~nd~~ are required. Expect the quality of s~~ervice~~ depend a bit on the level of crowding. tensive menu includes everything from omelets and giant cinnamon rolls for br~~eakfast~~ to every kind of salad and sandwich for and on up to prime rib and salmon for d~~inner~~ Whatever you order, you'll get hearty po~~rtions~~ of classic American food, perhaps with a Mexican twist here and there. In all hon~~esty~~ the food isn't the best you'll ever taste, bu~~t~~ good enough, it's hot, and it's plentiful.

Asian

Looking for a little Eastern flair with your dinner in the desert? Try **Wang's in the Desert** (424 S. Indian Canyon Dr., 760/325-9264, www.wangsinthedesert.com, $12–20). Friday evening happy hour tends to draw a big and mostly gay crowd, and likewise a group more interested in socializing than chowing down shows up to "Chill" on Sunday afternoons with a DJ spinning to help add to the atmosphere. But if you're looking for great Chinese food, you can find it here too. Take a seat on a banquette in the attractive gold and cream dining room and order from the distinctive menu. The dishes ring familiar, but Wang's puts its own stamp on the cuisine. You'll find unique appetizers and entrées that you won't taste anyplace else. Just be sure to get reservations at least a to **Native Foods** (1775 E. Palm Canyon Dr., Ste. F, 760/416-0070, www.nativefoods.com, Mon.–Sat. 11 A.M.–9:30 P.M., $8–15). This vegan restaurant offers a large menu of salads, sandwiches, soups, and hot food of all kinds, plus delicious desserts. You'll find some tasty seitan (a grain protein) faux meats and tempeh, as well as lots of bean dishes, veggie pizzas, and Middle Eastern–inspired cuisine. Native Foods even has a small kids' menu. This small SoCal chain also has a restaurant in Palm Desert (at 73–890 El Paseo Dr.) to satisfy the appetites of hungry vegan shoppers.

Coffee and Tea

Okay, so it's a chain. At least it's a Southern California regional chain. Still, the **Coffee Bean and Tea Leaf** (100 N. Palm Canyon Dr., 760/325-9402, $5) at the corner of Palm Canyon Drive serves up tasty coffee in a pleasant local atmosphere. You can get your favorite espresso drink and a pastry, and sit either inside or out to enjoy a quick breakfast.

INFORMATION AND SERVICES

Though it's the only one in the stark desert region, Palm Springs and its suburbs create a major urban center, and an affluent one at that. Expect to find all the goods and services you need and want someplace in or around Palm Springs.

Tourist Information

For newcomers to Palm Springs, a good first stop is the **Palm Springs Visitors Center** (777 N. Palm Canyon Dr., 760/778-8415, www.palm-springs.org). Here you'll get everything you need to enjoy your visit to the area, including real opinions on local attractions and restaurants. The website can help you even before you arrive—use it to select an inn, print up maps, and get the low-down on the best events and parties while you're in town.

Media and Communications

The local Palm Springs newspaper is *The Desert Sun* (www.mydesert.com). It's published daily and available at many local motels and restaurants, plus it's for sale at public newsstands and shops in all the various towns.

Cell phones work fine in Palm Springs, as do laptops with wireless Internet capability (though you'll often have to pay for the privilege to connect up).

All major American banks do business in Palm Springs, and you'll find a plethora of ATMs ready to help you access (and ultimately spend) your cash. Palm Springs and its satellite towns also have full-service **post offices**—at least one per town. The Palm Springs branch sits at 333 East Amado Road.

Medical Services

In a town full of retirees, medical care is easy to come by. If you need an emergency room, you'll definitely find one. Right in downtown Palm Springs, you can head for the **Desert Regional Medical Center** (1150 N. Indian Canyon Dr., 760/323-6511, www.desertmedctr.com), which provides both emergency and trauma care services. On the other hand, if you're looking for a plastic surgeon, the phone book can hook you up. I can't.

GETTING THERE AND AROUND
Air

The **Palm Springs International Airport** (3400 E. Tahquitz Canyon Way, 760/318-3800, www.palmspringsairport.com) offers flights with most major carriers and a few minor airlines. It is the only commercial airport in the region—if you can't fly into or out of here, you'll be driving in from the Los Angeles Basin. While the weather in Palm Springs is usually fabulous, when it gets bad it can shut down the whole airport, so keep that in the back of your mind when you plan your wintertime flights.

Bus

The **SunLine Transit Agency** (800/347-8628, www.sunline.org, adults $1, seniors $0.50) runs a number of bus lines throughout the Palm Springs region, running from Desert Hot Springs down through Palm Springs proper, into Indio and all the way down to Coachella and Thermal. Check out the route map online.

Car

Palm Canyon Drive is the main drag through downtown Palm Springs. Then it takes off and connects the back sides of all the other towns, from Palm Desert down to Indio. While it might sound like it, this drive isn't all that attractive unless you're really into strip malls and chain stores. There's little scenery otherwise.

If you're driving in from Los Angeles, I-10 is the most direct route east. I-10 runs through Palm Springs and down through Indio, out east past the south entrance of Joshua Tree.

Tours

If you love to go touring, you can find a variety of different styles and modes of transit in Palm Springs tours, self-guided or prepackaged. **Celebrity Tours** (760/770-2700, www.celebrity-tours.com, adults $35, children $14) offers two short city tours that focus on the (surprise) celebrity residents and their homes in the town of Palm Springs and in the connecting cities beyond. A luxury bus brings visitors to the homes of Bob Hope and Celine Dion, to the date farms at the edge of the urban center, then back to the Old Movie Colony of Palm Springs proper. You can also check out Celebrity's day trip tours into Los Angeles, Las Vegas, and other spots in the region.

The discerning boonie-crasher can check into **Adventure Hummer Tours** (760/285-0876, www.adventurehummer.com, adults $110–160, children $70–90). You'll board a militaristic H-1 Hummer for your open-air adventure out into the desert canyons beyond the city. Whether you want to see the remote off-road regions of Joshua Tree or check out the legendary earthquake-producing San Andreas Fault or both, Adventure Hummer can take you there.

If you prefer wait till after dark to head outside, check out **Sky Watcher Tours** (73–091 Country Club Dr., Ste. A42, Palm Desert, 760/831-0231, www.sky-watcher.com). You'll get an educational and entertaining tour of the night sky over the deserts surrounding Palm Springs that's perfect for kids and adults, plus fun takeaway sheets to help you identify constellations wherever (in the Northern Hemisphere) you are.

Joshua Tree

Joshua Tree National Monument and its namesake "trees" lies just east of Palm Springs and offers easy access from the Los Angeles area. The northern half of the park sits in the high-altitude Mojave Desert. But as the park's lands stretch south, they also dip down into the lower-set Colorado Desert. It's actually not too hard to see where the landscape starts to change; Joshua trees become fewer and fewer, while ocotillos and teddy bear cacti start to pop up in their place. Even the dust-dry ground changes in color and character, with the characteristic light tan boulders of the north country giving way to a darker gray ground in the south. While many visitors stick exclusively to the north end of the park, it's worth the time to drive the main park road south to check out a really different desert region.

SIGHTS
◖ Oasis of Mara

The best known and best visited oasis in Joshua Tree is undoubtedly the well-developed Oasis of Mara (Hwy. 62 and Utah Trail). A number of small springs well out of the ground along the Pinto Mountain fault here, providing the life-giving water that supports a large and lush (well, lush for the Mojave Desert) ecosystem. The earliest known residents of the Oasis were the Serrano people, who planted a new palm tree each time a boy was born, then used the products of those palm trees for tools,

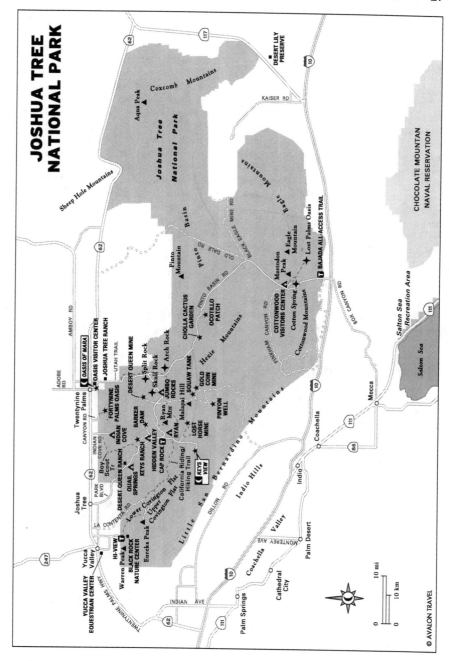

JOSHUA TREE NATIONAL PARK

© AVALON TRAVEL

shelter, and food. With the arrival of European-American settlers, the culture around the oasis and its surrounding grasslands changed. Gold mines sprang up, and ranchers brought in cattle to graze the region. One or two homes were even constructed here.

Today, over 100,000 people come through the Oasis visitors center just outside of the town of Twentynine Palms each year. Ironically, the Oasis sits outside the park boundaries, but it's still treated as a part of the park. A lovely easy nature trail loops around the oasis for half a mile. This wheelchair- and stroller-accessible trail includes a variety of signs that teach walkers about the natural features of the oasis. You'll see the palm trees, hardy grasses, and huge light boulders that characterize the region and hint at the beauty you'll find elsewhere in Joshua Tree.

Black Rock Canyon

West of the main entrances, just south of the tiny town of Yucca Valley, the Black Rock Canyon (Hwy. 247 at the northwest corner of the park) makes a great introduction to the park. The developed campground, nature and ranger center, and hiking trails are surrounded by the famed Joshua trees, which begin the spring bloom late each February. Lots of birds and mammals live nearby. You might see anything from a great horned owl to the threatened desert tortoise while you visit and camp here. You'll also see the famed black rocks that give the area its name. First-time visitors often walk the **Hi-View Nature Trail** (1.3 miles), a lovely interpretive stroll that points out and describes the plants and other natural features that characterize the northern Mojave Desert region of Joshua Tree National Monument. Black Rock Canyon also includes a trailhead for a 35-mile stretch of the California Riding and Hiking Trail and several other longer hiking trails. Check in at the ranger station for a wilderness permit if you plan to go on an overnight backpacking trip in the area.

Hidden Valley

One of the centerpieces of Joshua Tree, the

Joshua Tree

© LANCE SCOTT

Hidden Valley (Park Blvd., 10 miles south of West Entrance) offers hikes, a nature trail, a campground, and a rare view of a tiny desert valley. If you're day-tripping in Joshua Tree, park in the day lot and follow the tourists off to the right to the sort-of trail onto and through the big tan boulders. You'll scramble up, getting a great up-close view of the surprising granite mineral content of the pale boulders on either side of you. Emerge from the rocky trail into a small rocky meadowlike area, which includes small signs describing the natural features. Keep walking across the clearing and on to the next miniature pass.

Cap Rock and Skull Rock

Among the wonders of Joshua Tree are the fabulous boulder formations scattered about the landscape. As you drive or hike, especially in the northern reaches, you'll have a hard time missing at least a few of these great light orangeish-tan rocks. Sit and stare at them, thinking up different common animals and other things that the boulders and clusters resemble—kind of like cloud gazing, but without the movement.

Two rocks that are fairly close together by the road so resemble other objects that they're named and marked on park maps. If you take the east–west connecting road from Pinto Basin Road (the main north–south corridor) to the road to Keys View and Hidden Valley, you'll first pass Skull Rock (Park Blvd., seven miles east of Hidden Valley), one of the many giant stones that provide shade at the aptly named Jumbo Rocks campground. Guess what this rock is shaped like? Just past the intersection towards Hidden Valley, Cap Rock and its buddies offer interesting geology, a small picnic area, and a good spot for rock climbers to dig in and start scrambling.

Keys Ranch

The only way to get a real look at Keys Ranch (Keys Ranch Rd., Oct.–May Sat.–Sun. 10 A.M. and 1 P.M., adults $5, children $2.50) is to take a docent-guided tour of the buildings and land. William and Frances Keys were among the rugged settlers of the Mojave Desert. They ranched on the sparse desert grasses and raised five children on this patch that would become part of Joshua Tree. Today, visitors see the weathered pine buildings that housed the original ranch house, the schoolhouse that educated the few local children, the local general store, and a workshop. The orchard and landscaping have been replanted and revived. A collection of mining and farm equipment sits in the dry desert air, and relics like the old well dot the property here.

To get to Keys Ranch, drive half a mile north of the Hidden Valley campground, then turn off onto a bumpy one-lane dirt road (passenger cars okay) that runs for about a mile. Park near the gate and meet your tour guide just inside the property. Buying tickets in advance (you can call ahead and use a credit card) is recommended, especially on holiday weekends. If you're feeling lucky, you can just head up to the gate and ask the ranger if any spots are available on the next tour. Check the ranger schedule for weekday tours throughout the year.

◖ Keys View

One of the best views in all of Joshua Tree is the Keys View (end of Keys View Rd., bear right off Park Blvd. past Cap Rock). On a clear day, the view from here redefines the concept of "panoramic," letting travelers see the whole of the Palm Springs urban sprawl, the Coachella Valley farmland, the notorious San Andreas fault, and even the Salton Sea many miles to the southeast. You'll drive all the way to the end of the road out of the West Ranger Station, up to about 5,000 feet elevation and the sizeable parking lot. Get out of your car and climb a brief paved trail to the vantage point at the top of the ridge.

Sadly, crystal clear days are hard to come by. Not only is the ever-expanding Palm Springs cityscape polluting its valley, a pass to the west and prevailing winds often blow smog into the region from the Los Angeles Basin. The best time to catch a good view at Keys is the early morning, and the best way to help make the views better is to read the signs up on the path and do what you can to decrease your own emissions. Sure, you're only one person, but imagine what the mid-afternoon would look like at Keys View if even two out of three people did *only one person's* worth of responsible pollution reduction?

Cottonwood Spring Oasis

The Cottonwood Spring Oasis (Box Canyon Rd., turn onto spur road at visitors center) gets fewer visitors than many of the northern park sights, but it's one of the most beautiful oases in Joshua Tree. The catch? No Joshua

trees, because Cottonwood sits at the transitional area between the Mojave and Colorado Deserts. Instead, at the oasis you'll see a fabulous grove of desert fan palms, which are native to California. The thick growth of flora and fauna at this oasis is fed by Cottonwood Spring, a naturally occurring spring caused by the seismic activity in the region. (Caution: Do not drink the spring water! It's not potable.) The Cahuilla Native Americans used the spring water for washing, cooking, and more. They also hunted and gathered from the abundant natural resources here. You can still see

WHAT IS A JOSHUA TREE?

You'll see them everywhere in the north end of Joshua Tree National Park, and indeed they're common throughout much of the Mojave Desert. They do look almost like deciduous trees from a distance, and up close their foliage and "bark" looks like nothing else most folks have ever seen – spiky and scaly, green and brown and odd, with funky creamy greenish flowers every once in a while. It's definitely not a "regular" tree, but it doesn't look much like a cactus species either.

So what is a Joshua tree?

Desert botanists will probably figure out on their own that Joshua trees are members of the yucca family. Specifically, Joshua trees are *Yucca brevifolia* – a type of yucca that grows almost exclusively in the high-altitude (2,000-6,000 feet) Mojave Desert ecosystem. Though the trees can be delicate – they've got a shallow root system and all those branches get heavy – Joshua trees can live up to a thousand years.

If you get to see the Joshua trees bloom, you're lucky! They don't bloom every spring; it happens only when enough rain falls at the right time, and after the tree has experienced at least one hard freeze. Once they bloom, specially adapted yucca moths fertilize the flowers by laying eggs in them. This spreads pollen, and the blossoms turn into a greenish-brown fruit filled with seeds. The fruit drops, the seeds spread out on the ground and sprout, and new Joshua trees begin to grow.

You'll see other types of yucca plants throughout California, even in unlikely spots such as the Big Sur coast. Most of the common yuccas grow wider and closer to the ground than Joshua trees, and have much longer dagger-like leaves. Once you study their shape and the way the leaves grow, then the family resemblance becomes clear.

© LANCE SCOTT

evidence of their presence in left-behind artifacts. You'll also find the remains of more recent use of the spring: primitive, hand-built gold milling equipment left over from several 19th- and early 20th-century gold mills.

In the early springtime, the Cottonwood area leads the park's beautiful wildflower bloom with colorful desert dandelions, lupine, and others. Check in February for the first flowers. Any number of hiking trails encircle the area, perfect for day trips, and a campground offers rare shady spots with the sound of trickling water to lull you to sleep at night.

SPORTS AND RECREATION

Even more than the other California deserts, Joshua Tree invites outdoor sports enthusiast of all kinds into its wilderness to take advantage of the beauty and challenge of the diverse region. Whether you're a leave-no-trace backcountry backpacker, a hardcore climber, or a Jeep-driving boonie-crasher, you'll find your bliss here.

Hiking

Dozens of great hikes crisscross the length and breadth of Joshua Tree. Though many of these start in or near the visitors centers and developed campgrounds, don't neglect the trails that begin off the paved and unpaved roads of the park.

Before you begin a hike here—even a short two or three mile jaunt—be sure you're properly prepared. It's not as dry as Death Valley, but Joshua Tree National Monument is still a harsh and unforgiving desert. Bring lots of water (up to a gallon per person). For longer hikes, pack more water, food, and a first-aid kit. Talk to the rangers about safety, climate, and what to bring on a long day or multi-day backcountry adventure.

A number of trails start at the Black Rock Canyon campground. In addition to the **Hi-View Nature Trail,** many longer hikes begin here. To get to the summit of **Eureka Peak** (approx. 12 miles round-trip, difficult), first take the Burnt Hill Trail south to connect to the Eureka Peak Trail. You'll ascend 1,500 feet on this all-day trek up to some of the most

beautiful views in the whole park. Another option is the **Panorama Loop** (approx. 12 miles round-trip, difficult). Be sure to bring your camera!

Down south, the Cottonwood Spring area offers everything from quarter-mile nature walks to multi-mile intense hikes. If you're more into cactus than quadriceps strain, try the **Cholla Cactus Garden** (0.25 mile, easy). It's definitely worth it to spend the $0.50 on the descriptive pamphlet that will give you a greater understanding of the "jumping" cholla catci and the rest of the surrounding ecosystem. Look for the desert wood rats and cactus wrens that feed here, but be sure not to touch the pretty but vicious teddy bear cholla—the nasty little needles seem to jump off the cactus to bury themselves in unsuspecting hands.

Farther south, only half a mile from the park gate, the **Bajada All-Access Trail** (0.25 mile, easy) offers great views of the myriad plants that populate the Colorado Desert climate. As implied by the name, this nature trail is wheelchair-accessible.

For a longer and tougher hike, climb **Mastodon Peak** (3 miles round-trip, difficult). This steep hike takes you back up above 3,000 feet, where you'll take in views of Eagle Mountain and out to the Salton Sea. Check out the Mastodon Mind and the Winona Mill on your way. One of the longest and most rewarding hikes in this region takes you out to the **Lost Palms Oasis** (8 miles round-trip, difficult). Here grows the largest grove of fan palms in Joshua Tree, fed by natural year-round pools of fresh water.

Rock Climbing

Joshua Tree is one of the finest rock climbing parks in the United States, indeed in the world. Whether you're into bouldering or climbing, you'll find a plethora of climbing areas and routes here. The good climbing regions are almost all found in the northern reaches—the Mojave area, which is filled with granite canyons and fantastical boulder formations. Even the most dedicated of climbers can't chip the surface of Joshua Tree in just

LIZ HAMILL SCOTT ©

climbing Cap Rock

one trip, which is why many come back to the park year after year.

If you need equipment and supplies, the small towns along the north border of Joshua Tree support a number of climbing outfitters. Curious newcomers can even arrange guided climbs and climbing lessons through these companies. Obviously, **Joshua Tree Rock Climbing School** (760/366-4745, www.joshuatreerockclimbing.com, $120/one-day session) is prominent among these outfits. From one-day beginning seminars that teach the fundamentals of rock climbing up through four-day intensive sessions and lead climbing classes that take newbies up to the intermediate level in only half a week, this school offers a wonderful opportunity for aspiring climbers to start building their skills.

More than a dozen climbing spots surround the Indian Cove Campground. A tangle of paved roads service the area, and a large parking lot provides easy access to the boulders and cliff faces. Test your skills against Dos Equis Wall or Apparition Rock to the west, or Upper and Lower Dodge City to the south of the central camping area.

The climbing areas associated with the Hidden Valley are more spread out, but there are more of them and several of these range out into the wilderness area of the park. Near the parking area and campground you'll find The Real Hidden Valley Area, Cyclops, Echo Cove, and a number of others. Out to the northeast, you can hike or drive a dirt road out to Willow Hole to climb the Fortress, Super Dome, or Valley of Kings.

Between the Sheep Pass and Ryan campgrounds, several parking lots make it easy to stage climbs at Cap Rock, Hall of Horrors, and Love Nest. Other good places to stage climbs include the rough roads of the Geology Tour, the Queens Valley, and Split Rock.

Do be aware that strict rules govern climbing at Joshua Tree, and climbers are responsible for knowing those rules before they start up any boulders or steep faces. Be sure to check the park website or stop in at the ranger station to pick up a copy of those rules and the Fixed

Anchor Checklist. The website also offers top-ographical maps of the major climbing areas.

Horseback Riding

Several trails at Joshua Tree are open to equestrians as well as hikers. You can bring your own horse and ride the trails solo, or arrange with one of the local ranches to take a guided ride of the park and the area that surrounds it.

Joshua Tree Ranch (Park Blvd. Mile 2.9, 760/366-2788, www.joshuatreeranch.com, $65–125) offers easy rides on its own land just north of Joshua Tree, and moderately challenging rides into the park. You can also work with the ranch to create your own private ride for a higher fee. This ranch takes its horses and its riding quite seriously, so consider your real riding ability level and that of your companions and family before booking a ride with them. Reservations for all rides are required, but rides are available most days with enough advance warning.

A full-service equestrian center, the **Yucca Valley Equestrian Center** (7429 Avalon Ave., Yucca Valley, 760/365-4433, www.yuccavalley equestriancenter.com, $35/hour) leads easy rides across flat desert lands of Joshua Tree as well as more challenging rides through narrow canyons and up steep hills. While the standard trail tack is Western, you can request an English saddle when you reserve your ride.

If you'd rather strike out on your own, the most popular riding trail in Joshua Tree is the **California Riding and Hiking Trail.** This 35-mile section of what is actually a statewide trail has many access points throughout the north end of the park. Its park boundaries are the Black Rock Canyon campground (which includes a horse camp) in the west and the North Entrance Station to the east. You can see many of the most beautiful areas of Joshua Tree while riding this trail, many of which are not directly accessible by road. Ride through forests of Joshua trees and past amazing and rarely seen rock formations. You can do a two-day ride on this trail, stopping at the Ryan campground, which includes horse facilities, near the middle of the trail's length.

The 16-mile **Boy Scout Trail** also permits equestrian traffic. Running roughly from Indian Cove to Hidden Valley, it offers another scenic view of northern Joshua Tree for hikers and riders alike.

Off-Roading

Unlike many of California's wilderness parks, Joshua Tree welcomes off-road vehicles and provides more than half a dozen backcountry roads for four-wheel drives to bump out to explore otherwise inaccessible parts of the park. (Mountain bikes are also allowed on these roads, so keep a lookout while driving out there.)

One of the most popular backcountry roads is **Geology Tour Road** (Geology Tour Rd. and Park Blvd.). Pick up a printed road guide at the start of the road so you'll know about each of the 16 major geological (and other landscape) features you're looking at when you stop at them. In truth, during good years regular passenger cars (but not trailers and motor homes) can make part of this tour, from the turn off the main road to the Squaw Tank.

Queen Valley Roads are a network of smallish roads running for a total of about 13 miles. You'll get to see plenty of big granite boulders and Joshua trees as you bump along out here on the other side of the paved road from Hidden Valley. This makes a great mountain biking trek if you prefer to travel under your own steam.

In the south, several great roads offer a fun crash through the boonies of the Colorado Desert region of the park. The **Black Eagle Mine Road** (six miles north of Cottonwood visitors center) offers nine miles of scenic canyon vistas within the park boundaries, and BLM road and driveable side trails beyond. Outside of the park on the side roads, you'll come upon abandoned mines and old homesteads—beware of the dangerous and unstable mine shafts and equipment if you find them. Leading from the same cutoff, the **Old Dale Road** runs 23 miles through the Pinto Basin dry lakebed and up a steep mountain, then out of the park. More unstable mines and abandoned homes greet you once you cross the park boundary.

MOJAVE DESERT NATIONAL PRESERVE

California's Mojave Desert stretches for endless miles across the state. For the best views of the unique climate, formations, and ecosystem of this famous desert, visit the Mojave National Preserve (located btwn. I-15 and I-40, www.nps.gov, free). The Mojave is vast so don't expect to see all of the desert in one trip, even if you've got a whole week to spend. Pick your drives, hikes, and attractions carefully in order to see the Joshua Trees, caverns, cinder cones, and abandoned mines that most appeal to your interests.

The **Mojave Scenic Drive** is an easy day trip from Twentynine Palms or even Palm Springs. If you've only got one day, the best (and easiest) introduction to the Preserve is at the northern edge of the park along the smooth, well-kept pavement of I-15. From the town of Baker, turn south off I-15 onto Kelbaker Road for the 35-mile drive to Kelso. You'll traverse an alien landscape composed of volcanic activity, part of the Cinder Cones

National Natural Landmark. Stop in Kelso to explore the fabulous visitors center. The Spanish Revival facade of the **Kelso Depot Visitor Center** (Kelbaker Rd., Kelso, 760/252-6108, daily 9 A.M.-5 P.M.) welcomes travelers from all over the world. The visitor center once held the all-important Kelso Depot, which served the railroad that supported the many desert mining camps. The original structure has been renovated to include exhibits on the desert landscape and natural history, historically furnished dorm rooms, and a restored lunch counter. An abundance of park rangers are on hand with advice on yearly road conditions. (Not all roads are passable in standard cars each year. Be sure to ask here or at one of the other visitors centers about passable roads before striking out on your own.)

Snap a few photos of the Kelso Dunes along the horizon before climbing back into your car to turn onto Kelso-Cima Road. The road follows the Union Pacific rail line along the edge

---

If you're looking for a more serious adventure, the **Pinkham Canyon-Thermal Canyon Roads** is advised only for hardcore booniecrashers who know what they're doing and carry proper emergency supplies.

Mountain Biking

As of this book's publication, the only mountain biking allowed in Joshua Tree is along the backcountry roads shared with off-road vehicles. Check with the rangers at any of the visitors centers to learn whether 29 miles of designated mountain biking trails have opened by the time of your visit.

CAMPING

Many of the outdoors-loving visitors to Joshua Tree prefer to sleep out under the brilliantly glittering stars. If that's you, you've got your choice of mostly first-come campgrounds with tent and RV sites and at least basic facilities, and backcountry rough camping.

If you plan to backpack out into the

wilderness, you must register on one of the backcountry boards or get a permit at one of the ranger stations. Most of the major drive-in campsites have backcountry boards (bulletin boards where you can sign up and indicate your general planned route and destination.

At all the developed campgrounds, you must observe quiet hours, generator use restrictions, and deal with the lack of showers. In fact, only a few campgrounds offer any water at all. If you bring a solar shower, take care! The sun in this area can quickly give you a near-boiling shower experience.

The **Black Rock** (Black Rock Canyon, reservations Sept.–May 877/444-6777, $15) campground is one of the biggest and most developed in Joshua Tree. With 100 sites, running potable water, and full bathroom facilities, Black Rock offers a semblance of comfort in the harsh desert. Some spots take RVs, and the site has a dump station. Black Rock is one of the two park facilities where equestrians can camp with their horses.

of the Providence Mountains to the town of Cima, where you'll find snacks and drinks (but no gas). Cima also serves as a convenient fork; if you're in a hurry to get back to I-15, staying left on Cima Road will get you there the quickest. The right fork, **Morning Star Mine Road,** offers a more interesting route, including a turnoff to the abandoned mine that gives the road its name. From the mine, turn left onto Ivanpah Road and continue to Nipton Road to return to the freeway.

This drive takes about 90 minutes without stops, but feel free to hike the many great desert trails, photograph the Joshua Trees or the blossoming spring wildflowers, and explore (safely) an abandoned mine.

Planning to spend a weekend or longer exploring Mojave? For a total immersion into the desert world, spend your nights in one of the park's many campgrounds. **Hole-in-the Wall** campground is accessible from the Kelso-Cima Road and has toilet facilities, potable water, and an RV dump station. If your primary goal is to explore Mitchell Caverns, Hole-in-the-Wall's 37 campsites are closest to this major attraction.

Not too far from Hole-in-the-Wall, **Mid Hills** campground also has bathrooms, water, picnic tables, and fire rings for its 26 available sites. Like Hole-in-the-Wall, no reservations are accepted — all sites are first-come, first-served, so get there early during spring wildflower season. If you've come to Mojave to ride your horse through the beautiful and varied desert, make a reservation at the **Black Canyon** equestrian and group campground ($12, reservations 760/928-2572).

Want to camp all on your own, with no other campers nearby? Mojave has a number of existing roadside campsites that have sheltered independent desert-lovers for years. Just be sure to use an already existing site; look for stone fire rings and pre-disturbed earth to avoid further disturbing the fragile desert ecosystem.

The other horse-friendly campground is **Ryan** (Park Blvd. south of Hidden Valley, first-come, first-served, $10), which has more primitive facilities and fewer sites. Expect pit toilets and no available drinking or washing water here. Each site has a grate for cooking and campfires, and a picnic table.

Two other popular campgrounds, **Hidden Valley** (Park Blvd. south of West Entrance, first-come, first-served, $10) and **Jumbo Rocks** (Park Blvd. east of Geology Tour Rd., first-come, first-served, $10), sit near the center of the most traveled areas of the park. Both are primitive, with pit toilets and no water, but Jumbo Rocks has over 100 sites in great locations. Many of these sites sit beneath the shelter of boulders, a natural and historic way to camp. Both of these campgrounds are first-come, first-served. At Hidden Valley, RVs must be 25 feet or less.

Indian Cove (Indian Cove Rd. south of Entrance Station, reservations Sept.–May 877/444-6777, $15) offers over 100 campsites along the north park boundary in a location convenient to the small towns just north of Joshua Tree. While there's no water on-site, it's easy to come by at Joshua Tree and Twentynine Palms—and you can even get a hot meal in the evenings with only a short drive back to your tent! The Indian Cove area offers a half-mile nature trail for tourists who want to check out the local wildlife and traces of seasonal Native American settlements.

In the south of the park, **Cottonwood** (CA-195 at the Cottonwood Visitors Center, first-come, first-served, $15) offers water and flush toilets, as well as a dump station for RVs. The nearby visitors center offers a few basic supplies, and some of the loveliest hikes and wildflower viewings start in this region.

ACCOMMODATIONS

If you're looking for luxury in your accommodations, you'll need to stay in Palm Springs and day-trip in to Joshua Tree. A few town motels offer plain but clean and comfortable indoor beds just outside of the northern park boundary. Inside the park, your choices are campgrounds with flush toilets, campgrounds without flush toilets, and backcountry hike-to-it and do-it-yourself camping.

Most of the motel rooms adjacent to Joshua Tree lie in the town of Twentynine Palms. You'll find the usual array of national chains, plus a few independents vying for your business.

Under $100

Any U2 fans who've come to Joshua Tree to pay homage simply must stay at the **Harmony Hotel** (71161 29 Palms Hwy., 760/367-3351, www.harmonymotel.com, $77–95). This is where the band stayed when they were hard at work on the album named for the National Monument. It's a small, casual motel with only eight rooms total. The guest rooms have been recently remodeled, and you'll find white and light-patterned linens, cute sitting and dining areas in the larger rooms, and original artwork in each room. Pick a room with a king or two double beds, request one of the rooms with a kitchenette, or make yourself a pot of coffee in the guests' kitchenette/break room. Be sure to take a break in either the piping-hot outdoor spa in the evening or the deliberately unheated pool in the heat of the summer's day. For a quick break from the natural wonders, take in the artwork that surrounds the inn.

$100-150

Sunnyvale Garden Suites Hotel (73843 Sunnyvale Dr., Twentynine Palms, 760/361-3939, www.sunnyvalesuites.com, $100–190) is perfectly located downtown, but off the noisy highway, in Twentynine Palms. Don't let the rugged exterior with its Western-style weathered pine boards fool you—the interiors feature comfortable modern amenities. All rooms have vintage tubular brass-style or wooden bedsteads, simple and soothingly colored linens and curtains, and plenty of space. Rooms sleep 2–6 people, and some have full kitchens. Outside of the guest room, enjoy the fitness center and the large outdoor spa, or take a walk in the climate-appropriate desert garden that surrounds the property. Bring the kids out

to the playground in the cool mornings and evenings to burn off some energy, or just take a family stroll around the residential neighborhood of Twentynine Palms.

A favorite with repeat visitors, the **Circle C Lodge** (6340 El Ray Ave., Twentynine Palms, 760/367-7615, www.circleclodge.com, $135–150) offers lovely accommodations away from the noisy center of town and out in the desert. Choose from a guest room with a king bed or two queens; each room has its own well-equipped kitchenette (all the kitchen lacks is an oven). Light, floral decor with colorful blue and red accents and TVs with VCRs (but no DVD players just yet) make the oversized rooms pleasant and homey. Each morning head down to the courtyard for a complimentary bagel with fresh fruit, juice, and coffee. The sparkling pool and cute circular shaded spa invite visitors to relax after a dusty day of hiking at Joshua Tree.

$150-250

Roughley Manor (74744 Joe Davis Dr., Twentynine Palms, 760/367-3238, www.roughley manor.com, $150–185) seems to be poorly named; this lovely B&B is anything but rough, inside or out. Once the homestead of a young couple named Campbell who dreamed of ranching in the desert, the inn now welcomes guests all year long. With a dozen rooms, two in the lovely stone-clad main house and the rest in a handful of other buildings scattered throughout the large garden property, Roughley offers more space and better privacy than most similar inns. Each individually decorated guest room uses floral themes as they should be used—sparingly—to create the sense of a guest suite in a private elegant farmhouse. Many of the suites have kitchenettes and dining areas to create an additional sense of staying at home rather than at an impersonal motel. The prices are amazingly cheap if you're accustomed to the B&Bs of the big cities and Wine Country, and the location is perfect for sojourns out into Joshua Tree.

FOOD

There's no food inside Joshua Tree National Park. Picnickers and campers must pack in every bite of food they intend to eat. The only visitors centers that maintain snack bars reside just outside the park boundaries.

Multi-night campers sometimes long for a hot meal served by someone else at a clean table. If that's what you need, you can drive into Twentynine Palms or even Palm Springs for a tasty meal.

Restaurants

The most talked-about eatery adjacent to Joshua Tree is the **Crossroads Cafe & Tavern** (61715 29 Palms Hwy., Joshua Tree, 760/366-5414, www.crossroadscafeandtavern.com, Sun.–Tues. 6:30 A.M.–8 P.M. Thurs.–Sat. 6:30 A.M.–9 P.M., $5–10). It sure doesn't look like much from the outside, with its rusted aluminum siding and bright blue painted trim. But it's what's inside that counts, and inside the Crossroads you'll find friendly owners running their own place with the assistance of a tiny tribe of well-trained employees. The food is as unpretentious and tasty as the owners. At breakfast you can get an array of egg dishes, while lunch and dinner run to salads and sandwiches. The price is right at the Crossroads, so you won't break the bank for a reasonably health conscious meal here. Plenty of vegetarian options dot the menu, though carnivores aren't left out either.

Longing for a gooey slice of pizza or a big ol' hearty sub? Try **Sam's Pizza** (61380 29 Palms Hwy., Joshua Tree, 760/366-9511, www.samspizza.com, Mon.–Thurs. 11 A.M.–8 P.M., Fri.–Sat. 11 A.M.–7 P.M., Sun. 3–8 P.M., $5–20). The big menu features an array of reasonably priced Italian and American dishes that are perfect after a long day of hiking or climbing. Create your own pizza, or go for a classic hot meatball sub. If you're planning a late afternoon in the park, order cold subs and have them wrapped up to go. Specialties include calzones, paninis, and even a few Greek dishes beckon, while full-sized dinners appeal to seriously hungry diners.

Decent and inexpensive Mexican cuisine in the Joshua Tree desert region is served at **Santana's Mexican Food** (73680 Sun Valley Dr., Twentynine Palms, 760/361-0202, open daily, $5–10). Grab a burrito, a couple of tacos, or even a combo plate here, and top it off with an offering from the open salsa bar. Yum!

Cafés

The **Park Rock Café** (6554 Park Blvd., Joshua Tree, 760/366-3622, Mon.–Sat. 9 A.M.–6 P.M., Sun. 9 A.M.–4 P.M., $10–20) serves casual café food and espresso drinks next door to the Joshua Tree Visitors Center near the West Entrance to the park. Park Rock is a good place to grab a quick bite before entering the park or just after leaving.

Markets

Need to stock up on groceries before hitting the park? Two local markets can supply hungry hikers and campers in need of supplies. **Stater Bros** (58060 29 Palms Hwy., Yucca Valley, 760/365-2415) sits near the western entrances. Near the Oasis entrance, check out the **Plaza Market** (5668 Historic Plz., Twentynine Palms, 760/367-3464).

INFORMATION AND SERVICES
Tourist Information

It's hard to drive more than a dozen miles in Joshua Tree without tripping over a ranger station or a nature center. Most of these are tiny, but they're prolific and you'll get the information you need wherever you stop. If you're camping at any of the larger campgrounds, you'll probably find a nature center somewhere in it.

The **Oasis Visitors Center** (760/367-5500, year-round daily 8 A.M.–5 P.M.) sits at the Oasis of Mara. It's got all you need in terms of rangers, a bookshop, special exhibits including videos, and more.

West of the Oasis, you can enter the park at the **Joshua Tree Visitors Center** (760/366-1855, year-round daily 8 A.M.–5 P.M.). A fun little interpretive museum explains the origins and current fun available in Joshua Tree, and knowledgeable rangers can inundate you with maps and advice. Day-trippers often grab a quick bite and some extra water from the adjoining café before heading into the foodless desert park.

If you're entering the park from I-10 in the

south, your first stop will be the **Cottonwood Visitors Center** (no phone, year-round daily 9 A.M.–3 P.M.). This tiny center has maps and rangers, a picnic ground, and flush toilets and running water, but very little else.

Media and Communications

The National Park publishes several pamphlets and papers for visitors. Ask for these at any of the visitors centers.

In an emergency, call **San Bernardino dispatch** (909/383-5651). Cell phone coverage is unreliable in the park, especially in the backcountry. Don't depend on your cell phone in cases of emergency. You can find public phones at the Joshua Tree and Oasis visitors centers.

You won't find Internet access inside the park. You might find a Wi-Fi connection at your motel in Twentynine Palms, and there's certainly plenty of Internet in Palm Springs.

The Twentynine Palms **post office** is located at 73839 Gorgonio Drive.

Medical Services

For non-emergency medical needs, the nearest place to find a wide variety of clinics open at all hours is Palm Springs. In an emergency, dial 911 or 909/383-5651 (San Bernardino dispatch).

GETTING THERE AND GETTING AROUND
Air

The nearest major airport to Joshua Tree is at **Palm Springs** (3400 E. Tahquitz Canyon Way, 760/318-3800, www.palmspringsairport. com). It only takes about an hour to drive from the airport out to the park.

Car

You can drive from Palm Springs or even Los Angeles to the south entrance of Joshua Tree on I-10. From I-10 heading east, turn north (left) onto Box Canyon Road, which takes you right up to the Cottonwood Springs Visitors Center.

To enter at the north side of the park, find your way to Twentynine Palms Highway, also known as State Highway 62. Highway 62 originates at I-10 northwest of Palm Springs, or to avoid the freeway take Indian Avenue up through Desert Hot Springs and around to the north side of the park. From Highway 62, you can turn in to Black Rock Canyon, the Joshua Tree Visitors Center, or the Oasis of Mara.

Parking inside Joshua Tree usually isn't too difficult, as ample parking lots are provided for the major attractions. On holiday weekends, come early for the best spots and least crowded hikes.

Death Valley

For a valley famed for its uncompromising climate, Death Valley teems with life. Desert plants, including funky pickleweed and more common creosote, wildflowers, and even desert-dwelling fish and snails live here in profusion. Even the rocks, cliffs, salt flats, and mountains seem to live and breathe here. The best way to experience the amazing world that is Death Valley is to visit for at least a weekend, driving from sight to sight and then getting out of the car to walk out into the desert.

SIGHTS
◀ Scotty's Castle

If you ask the locals around Death Valley if

there's one single thing not to miss, almost to a person they will tell you to see Scotty's Castle (Hwy. 267 in Grapevine Canyon, 3 miles northeast of Grapevine intersection, adults $11). The unfinished grand Spanish-styled home is the only private mansion ever built in Death Valley. Contrary to popular legend, it never was the home of infamous huckster Death Valley Scotty—he actually lived in a rough cabin on the property, only hanging out in the castle with his friend Albert Johnson. In truth, the mansion was built and furnished by Johnson and his wife, a wealthy couple from Chicago who initially invested in Scotty's oft-lauded but never seen gold mine but became

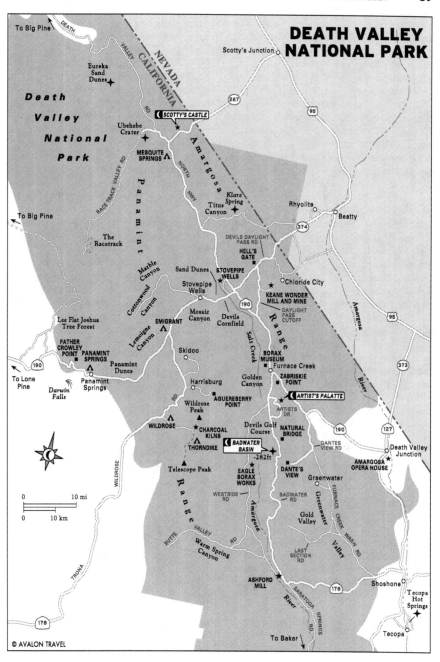

© AVALON TRAVEL

close friends to Scotty anyway. The Johnsons and Scotty often entertained at the castle, and movie stars and presidents came to stay in the guest rooms here. Once upon a time, you could have even rented one of the upstairs guest rooms by the week.

Today, several different tours give visitors different glimpses into the wonders of Scotty's Castle. For first-time visitors, docents recommend the regular main-house tour. If you've already been through the castle proper, consider the Underground Mysteries tour. Purchase tickets at the ticket booth (the first building as you enter the attraction's center). A good place to start while you wait for your tour time is the visitors center and interpretive museum, which describes the history of the castle, Death Valley Scotty, and Albert Johnson. Your tour will meet at the fountain in front of the castle entrance. All tours are conducted by Park Service employees who dress and speak as though it were still the late 1930s and you were friends of Johnson and Scotty come to dine and stay at the castle. The highlight of the tour is the magnificent player organ in the music room, which still plays for visitors every day. (Check with the visitors center for musical events at the castle.)

Once you've finished your tour, you can wander the property, climbing up a little hill to visit Scotty's grave. You'll also see the remains of the construction facilities—the building of the castle was never finished—you'll notice the empty swimming pool and some half-built exterior structures scattered about. If you'd like to buy souvenirs or a quick snack, you can do so at Scotty's Castle, which also has restroom facilities.

◖ Badwater Basin

Want to go down—all the way down to the lowest land on the continent? Drive out and follow the signs from Highway 190 to Badwater Basin (Hwy. 178, 18 miles south of Furnace Creek, turn off 190 onto 178 at Furnace Creek Inn). At 281 feet *below* sea level, Badwater holds the title of the lowest elevation in the Western Hemisphere. Tourists love to get their photos taken beside the elevation sign sitting out on the boardwalks that protect the tiny salt pond here. Please respect this pond; its ecosystem is frail and includes a species of snail found nowhere else in the world, and you can damage it just by walking up to its edge. Keep to the boardwalk as you gaze into the water that seems impossible in the blinding heat of the salt flats of this long-dried-out lakebed. You can walk off the boardwalk and out onto the salt flats; just follow the obviously human-created path. Ahead of you, the western mountain range might boast a coating of snow during the winter months, and the view up the valley is astonishing on a clear day. Also be sure to turn around and take a look up at the mountains just behind you. See if you can spot the Sea Level sign way up the hillside.

But be careful, since even in the wintertime the ground beneath you on the salt flats can be up to 80°F hotter than the air around you. Yes, the rubber soles of your shoes can melt right into the salt on a warm day! The National Park rangers beg you not to go to Badwater in the summertime. The danger is very real and trying to explore the salt flats in the summertime can be fatal. Even in the wintertime, bring water with you to this region, especially if you plan to go hiking here. Though there's no visitors center at Badwater, you will find potable water at the restrooms adjacent to the parking lot. Expect to find plenty of other cars in that parking lot, as Badwater is one of the most popular spots to visit in Death Valley.

◖ Artist's Palette

Perhaps the single most classically beautiful spot in Death Valley, the Artist's Palette (Artists Drive, turn off Hwy. 178 about 7 miles south of Furnace Creek) almost looks like some sort of manmade trick. It seems so improbably that all those brilliant colors splashed together in one spot can really be a random conglomeration of different minerals all clustered in this one spot. But if you look carefully at the mountains elsewhere in Death Valley, you'll find examples of all the colors in the Palette throughout. Even along the Artist's Palette

© LANCE SCOTT

Artist's Palette

cutoff, swaths of color spill down the mountains for miles through the narrow canyon. It's worth your time to slow down on the road, even to stop and photograph some of the "secret" painted spots.

The one-way road through Artist's Palette splits off from Highway 178 and runs for about five miles (entrance at the south side), and the road is paved and driveable by regular cars. The best time to hit the Palette is just before sunset, when the falling sun limns the already amazing colors with gold. You'll see bunches of people pulled off the road and walking up and down a rise to take photos of a colorful cliff, but this is *not* the Palette proper. Stop to look, but then keep driving until you see the Artist's Palette sign and turn right into the drive for the parking lot. Walk a few steps up a tiny rise and you'll see the Palette right in front of you in all its pastel glory. You'll also see a number of other tourists at all times of day. No restrooms or water are available at Artist's Palette.

Devil's Golf Course

One of the eeriest formations in Death Valley is the ground at Devil's Golf Course (Hwy. 178 about 11 miles south of Furnace Creek). This part of the low salt flat that was the bottom of a long-vanished lake got stirred up somehow. The results are spectacular, with acre upon acre of chewed-up ground covered with delicate crystalline salt formations. It's a good idea to wear long pants and sturdy shoes and to be very careful if you plan to walk out onto the Golf Course. The ruts, holes, and crevices can be knee-deep, rocks and crystals are razor-sharp, and to call the walking "uneven" is the understatement of the year. If you're a photographer, be sure to bring your camera to capture the fragile salt crystal growths proliferating here.

Yes, every step you take out onto Devil's Golf Course destroys countless beautiful crystals. So why does the park let you walk out there? Because these crystals aren't a permanent feature of the region. Every time it rains, the crystals melt down to a salty liquid, then as the Golf Course dries out, the crystals start growing anew.

The road in to Devil's Golf Course is dirt and can get rough, but it's passable by passenger car. The slower you drive, the better condition the road will stay in. There's a parking lot in the Golf Course and a couple of plaques describing the formation and geology of the area. However, there are no restrooms or water here.

Dante's View

One of the many glorious views of Death Valley can be accessed by car at Dante's View (end of Dante's View Rd., turn off Hwy. 190 about 10 miles southeast of Furnace Creek). From more than a mile high, you can look out over what feels like the whole valley—right down into the salt flats of Badwater, up to Furnace Creek, and beyond. Right next door you can wave at the thematically named Coffin Peak to the south of Dante's. As the main views spread out to the west, Dante's Peak is a great place to watch the sun set over Death Valley.

Salt Creek

You may have heard of the famous Death Valley pupfish, a species of fish that lives in only one spot on the globe—here at Salt Creek (Hwy. 190, about 15 miles north of Furnace Creek, turnoff on west side of the highway). It's a strange contradiction, with a shining creek flowing through some of the most dry and desolate landscape on Earth. Toward the center of the valley off Highway 190, Salt Creek runs all year, its source a small spring, its terminus the hard ground where a miniature delta spreads out then dries up. To protect the delicate ecosystem in and around the heavily salinated creek, the Park Service has built a boardwalk that lets visitors see the plants, algae, and pupfish without treading on and in the delicate landscape here. The boardwalk runs from the parking lot up to the area where the pupfish spawn early in the wintertime. As spring comes, the pupfish swim downstream, making viewing easy even for visitors who don't want to take a hike. All around the boardwalk you'll see plants that thrive on salty water, including the funky pickleweed. That's the big bushy plant with the succulent-like tentacles divided into small greenish-orange droplets.

This plant is so salty that early pioneers in the area used it to make pickles instead of adding salt—hence its name.

The drive from the highway is about two miles on a dirt road that's passable in a passenger car. Pit toilets sit in the parking lot area. The boardwalk trail is wheelchair accessible.

Ubehebe Crater

Just about every type of major geological feature was once a part of the Death Valley landscape. In the north end of the valley, a recent (in geologic time) volcano left behind Ubehebe Crater (8 miles west of Scotty's Castle, from Hwy. 190 take left fork at the Grapevine). A quick walk up from the parking lot takes you right to the edge of the crater, which consists of razor-sharp black volcanic rock that is on the opposite inner face of the crater fading into a bright salmon pink and even a stark white. The view over the edge of the crater back down the valley is worth coming up here, and when you turn around you see the less visited but also lovely north end of the valley. Ubehebe is a great place to go hiking if you're in good shape—among other things, you can climb up from the parking area along the crater's rim to Little Hebe crater, a smaller crater created by the same volcano about 2,000 years ago.

Get to Ubehebe Crater by taking the other fork at the intersection that takes you to Scotty's Castle. The road is easily traversable by passenger cars; there's a parking lot but no restroom or water here.

Museums

In the town of Furnace Creek, out by the Ranch, you'll find two tiny museums that give guests a deeper understanding of both the natural and human history of Death Valley. The **Borax Museum** (admission free) at Furnace Creek Ranch focuses on the mining history of the area, with a tiny interior gallery/bookshop filled with mineral samples, books and documents, and smaller mining tools. The bulk of the museum sits outdoors, displaying an array of desiccated large mining and support equipment. Get a map indoors for $1 that

© LANCE SCOTT

Borax Museum

describes each numbered exhibit outside. You'll see hand-built mining machines, carriages and wagons, a steam locomotive, and more.

Just a few yards north of the Ranch sits the **Furnace Creek Visitors Center and Museum** (Hwy. 190 at the gas station, 760/786-3200, year-round daily 9 A.M.–5 P.M.). The interpretive museum here tells the story of Death Valley's long, slow formation and erosion. Even if you're not a rock nut, it's worth your time to stop in here to learn more about the natural wonders you'll witness when you get out on the road to explore. This is also a good spot to talk to rangers about the relative passability of the various rugged roads in the park, and to learn about the very real dangers of exploring Death Valley and how to keep yourself as safe as possible during your journey.

ENTERTAINMENT AND EVENTS

The main entertainment in Death Valley are the sights and (lack of) sounds of the valley itself. If you're an energetic night owl, plan to enjoy full-moon hikes rather than dance clubs, since you can count the number of saloons in the whole of the valley on one hand.

Bars and Clubs

For a drink or two to cap off a long day out in the desert, head on down to the **Corkscrew Saloon** at Furnace Creek Ranch (Hwy. 190 at Furnace Creek, 760/786-2345, daily noon–midnight). Go ahead and wear your boots and hat into the cowboy-styled bar with its wood floor and dim lighting. Drink a mug of beer on tap, grab a glass of wine, or sip your favorite cocktail from the full bar. They've got a TV with the game on for sports fans, and a pool table for desert sharks. The crowd mixes the ubiquitous tourists and a few die-hard locals who serve as the Corkscrew's regulars.

The other local watering hole sits a little north of Furnace Creek: the **Badwater Saloon at Stovepipe Wells** (Hwy. 190 past the big bend, 760/786-2387, daily 5:30 P.M.–9 P.M.). Attached to the Toll Road Restaurant, this saloon has beer, wine, cocktails, and a small snack menu to satisfy evening munchers over 21. It's not open too late, so you'll need to get your quaffing in early in the evening.

Live Music

Outside the park proper in the town of Amargosa Valley, Nevada, you'll find one of the most original entertainments available anywhere at the **Amargosa Opera House** (Death Valley Junction, 760/852-4441, www.amargosa-opera-house.com, adults $15, children $12). This lovely small theater is the pride and joy of Marta Beckett, a dancer from New York City who found her "home" in an abandoned theater in Death Valley Junction, where her car was getting a flat tire fixed. She and her husband repaired and renovated the theater, creating an intimate space where Marta could perform for an appreciative, if small, audience. That was in 1968. In the early 1970, Marta was inspired to paint murals on the walls and ceiling of her Opera House—a permanent audience for her ballets.

It's been 40 years, and Marta still dances at the Opera House each Saturday night from November through the middle of May. Reservations are required, as the seating is limited and Marta's shows often sell out. The show you see was created and choreographed by Marta, incorporating music, ballet, and comedy. The best way to learn about these unique entertainments is to see one for yourself.

You can also stay at the Amargosa if you like, since the old adobe hotel building has been renovated and is open to guests all year long. You can even ask for one of the rooms in which Marta has painted some of her lovely murals.

Festivals and Events

The Death Valley mythos—a place where intrepid miners and hardy pioneers couldn't find water and sought to leave ASAP—wouldn't be complete without an annual tribute to those first white visitors. The **49er Encampment** (www.deathvalley49ers.org) takes place throughout the first week of November each year. Thousands of history buffs flock to the

valley to camp, tell stories, sing songs, dance, and take tours of the park. Participants and guests alike enjoy the parade, which is one of the highlights of the many activities put on by the Encampment.

SPORTS AND RECREATION

The outdoor recreation comprises much of Death Valley's attraction to the million visitors the park sees each year. Whether you're an extreme sandboarder, an aggro four-wheeler, or a slow walker, you'll find something worth doing out-of-doors in Death Valley.

Off-Roading

If you've got a 4x4, or you know how to drive one and can rent one, it's well worth it to bring a hardy off-road vehicle into Death Valley. Many of the off-the-beaten-track sights and trails can only be accessed by high-clearance and four-wheel-drive vehicles.

The drive out to the **Natural Bridge** (about 1 mile off Hwy. 190, 1–2 miles south of Devil's Golf Course) isn't long or aggressive, but the road condition makes high-clearance or 4WD a good idea in most seasons. Check with the rangers for current conditions. Once you park, you've got a half-mile walk in to see the magnificent stone arch stretching across yet another beautiful desert canyon.

One of the most out-of-the-way sights in the park is **The Racetrack** (27 miles from Ubehebe Crater). You'll take a 27-mile drive on an incredibly rough road out to a patch of desert where a mysterious (but explicable) phenomenon draws hardy visitors out beyond the crowded main valley sights. You don't really need to hike anywhere—just get out of your car and stare out across the plateau at the deep grooves in the barren lakebed. The tracks are made by rocks sliding across the lakebed. See a track with no rock at the end of it? Sadly, uncaring tourists often pick up the rocks and take them home. Please leave the rocks where nature put them to allow future visitors to enjoy the unusual sight.

Also in the north end of the valley, the **Eureka Dunes** (10 miles south of Big Pine

Rd.) are some of the most unusual dunes you'll ever see, no matter how far you travel. The sand composing the dunes is the only sand nearby, and it rises 700 feet off the valley floor. You can walk up the Eureka Dunes, but no horseback riding and sandboarding aren't allowed here. This is a measure to protect the delicate ecosystem that evolved right here at the dunes and exists nowhere else on Earth. The drive runs about 40 miles or so, first on a long unpaved road running north from the Y-intersection to Scotty's Castle, then on a 4WD track about 10 miles to the dunes. Out towards the dunes, sand can get deep, so rangers recommend that *experienced 4WD drivers only* attempt this road.

The lovely **Titus Canyon** (Hwy. 190 about 20 miles north of Stovepipe Wells intersection) can be traversed on foot or by a 26-mile one-way 4WD track that connects directly to the ghost town of Rhyolite. Along the many miles of canyon, you'll see some of the most diverse and arguably most beautiful desert canyon scenery anywhere in Death Valley. It's got Native American petroglyphs, bighorn sheep, colorful mineral deposits, and skinny "narrows" where the walls soar overhead and almost black out the sun. Because the 4WD road runs only one way, you must come back into Death Valley by making a long loop into Nevada. Take Highway 374 past Rhyolite to Highway 95. Head either north to Highway 267, which will take you back to Scotty's Castle, or south to Highway 373 through Amargosa Valley, which becomes 127, then turn onto 190 which takes you back to Furnace Creek. Consider making your viewing of Titus Canyon an all-day adventure.

Out west in the Panamint Springs area, take your truck on a drive up to **Aguereberry Point** (Emigrant Canyon Rd. about 13 miles south of Emigrant intersection). This drive includes passing the ghost town of Harrisburg—an early 20th-century gold mining town that once had a population of 300 living in tents. You can actually walk right into this mine, which has been stabilized and made safe for visitors to spelunk in. Just be sure that the mine isn't closed to protect hibernating bats. All the way up the road, park and climb up to the point, which provides more beautiful valley vistas to enjoy. If you're staying in Panamint Springs, Aguereberry Point makes a good sunset or sunrise destination.

Hiking

Though you can reach most of the major sights of Death Valley by driving and perhaps a short walk, to get off the beaten track you'll need to take a hike. In fact, that's why many visitors come here. The best time to hike in the floor of Death Valley is the wintertime, when temperatures are cool to moderate. On the other hand, if you're interested in hiking the high country, the best time to explore the ridges is in the summer when the snow has melted.

For a fun easy or moderate walk where you can control both the distance and the elevation change, park on the side of the road and wander on out to the **Sand Dunes** (2–4 miles round-trip, easy) near Stovepipe Wells. The dunes are constantly shifting, and regular visitors love them because they're never the same two years in a row. They're beautiful at sunset when the golden light hits them, and if you're visiting during a full moon you'll find few more romantic spots to share an outdoor stroll with your sweetie.

From the roadside parking area, just walk out toward the cluster of dunes. They look like they're only a few yards away, but the desert air creates false senses of distance and it's about a mile to the edge of the dunes. There's no trail. You can walk right up the sides of the dunes. The hundreds of pockmark-like footprints bear witness to other visitors' climbs. If you climb as far as you can up the tallest dune, the round-trip is four miles.

Mosaic Canyon (1–4 miles round-trip, moderate) offers a variable length and difficulty hike with beautiful rock formations that resemble mosaics. Check out the canyon walls on the first half-mile of the walk for the best mosaics. If you want to, you can continue a couple of miles farther into the canyon. This hike starts at the Mosaic Canyon parking lot, a couple of miles past Stovepipe Wells Village.

If you don't have a 4x4 vehicle but you want to see the charming **Titus Canyon Narrows** (3–13 miles round-trip, easy), you can leave your car at the Titus Canyon parking lot and walk down the unpaved road. The Narrows go on for about a mile and a half of level road—if you're up for a much longer walk, you can get all the way to Klare Springs and the local petroglyphs.

For a scenic summer walk, **Dante's Ridge** (1–8 miles, moderate) offers soaring vistas and cool temperatures even in July. If you want a short hike, climb 0.5 mile from the Dante's View parking lot to the first peak in the chain. If you're done, feel free to walk back down; if you're feeling energetic, keep descending and climbing the ridge to the top of Mount Perry. You'll need to be an adventurous sort, as there's no trail past the first peak, though hiking is allowed.

Bring a detailed map if you plan to take on the hike through **Fall Canyon** (6 miles round-trip, difficult). Start at the Titus Canyon parking lot and from there, head north along a trampled path, and from there you're on your own as you descend a wash into the canyon and to a "dryfall." If you're up to it, you can skirt around the dryfall and head down to the most spectacular narrows area of the canyon.

If you're into the mining history of Death Valley, the **Keane Wonder Mine Trail** (2 miles, difficult) is a must-hike. It's a rough go—steep and rocky the whole mile up from the ruins of the mill to the ruins of the mines. Ruin crawlers will love the whole area. When the Keane Wonder Mine ceased production, it was abandoned and has been slowly desiccating ever since. At the top of the trail, you'll find the abandoned and incredibly dangerous mine entrances. The Park Services begs you not to enter these unstable structures. Be sure to take a break from the mines to look out over the whole of Death Valley from your perch.

If you're an aggro hiker visiting Death Valley in the summertime, check out **Telescope Peak Trail** (14 miles round-trip, difficult). The trail begins at the Mahogany Flat Campground and climbs 3,000 feet to the peak of the tallest mountain in Death Valley. The sweeping views will take what's left of your breath away after your climb. The snow usually melts by the beginning of June; if you want to try this trail in the winter you'll need an ice axe, crampons, and lots of previous winter climbing experience.

Biking

You've got to be pretty tough to bring your bike to a place called Death Valley. But plenty of folks do. The main biking road is Highway 190, which runs north–south along the east side of the valley. You can cut off the highway onto any paved road if you want to take in some sights. However, no bikes are allowed off the pavement in Death Valley.

Horseback Riding

At Furnace Creek Ranch (Hwy. 190, 760/786-2345, www.furnacecreekresort.com), you can take a horseback ride out into the desert from October through May. Horse-and-carriage rides are also available on occasion. Call the ranch or ask at the front desk for more information and to make reservations.

Golf

It's not a golfing destination, but if you're just burning to play a round in the hottest valley on earth, book a tee time at the **Furnace Creek Ranch Golf Course** (Hwy. 190, 760/786-2345, www.furnacecreekresort.com/golf-1203.htm, green fee $30–55, cart rental $12.50). Nope, it's not the shining green you'll find at most golf courses, for obvious reasons. Even in winter, limited water can be spared to irrigate greens and fairways. This 18-hole, par 70 course is part of the Furnace Creek Ranch complex near the center of Death Valley. You'll find restaurants and a general store at the Ranch. Check the website for golf and lodging packages.

CAMPING

Folks who want to explore Death Valley on the cheap quickly the fill the campsites that dot the park. Whether you're in an RV or just have a tent to pitch, you'll find someplace that suits your fancy. Just be aware that during high season (winter), the popular central campgrounds fill up fast. You can make reservations for a spot at many of the popular campgrounds by calling 877/444-6777 or online at www.recreation.gov. During the summer, camping in Death Valley can be extremely unpleasant, since few campgrounds here offer shade of any kind to take the edge off the extreme heat. Camping from June to September is not recommended in the lowland areas, and many campgrounds are closed from May to September.

RV and Tent Campgrounds

RV campers love to hang out in Death Valley. Accordingly, several full hook-up RV campgrounds offer space to settle in for a stay.

Both on the same side as the ranch and across the road, **Furnace Creek** (Hwy. 190 at Furnace Creek, 800/365-2267, www.furnacecreekresort.com, open year-round, $12–18) offers both RV spaces and tent camping. Campers gain access to the facilities at the Ranch, including the swimming pool, golf course, restaurants, and store. The RV camping sits mostly on the opposite side of Highway 190 from the Ranch, and the "campground" is in fact a stretch of barren asphalt with no shade whatsoever. This campground fills up fast during the busy winter months and you must make a reservation to get a spot here. Expect to find running water, flushies, and fireplaces at or near your site.

If you want to camp near, but not in, Furnace Creek Ranch, you can choose between **Texas Springs** (east of Furnace Creek, $12) and **Sunset** (east of Furnace Creek, north of Texas Springs, $10). Both are open from October through April, and feature running water, flush toilets, and RV dump stations. Of the two, Texas Springs has the nicest amenities, with picnic tables and fire rings. Both campgrounds are wheelchair accessible.

Another popular RV park sits at the tiny villagelet of **Stovepipe Wells** (Hwy. 190 at Stovepipe Wells, 760/786-2387, open Oct.–Apr., $12). Again, you get access to the small general store and the tavern if you park on the wide patch of asphalt here. There are also several fun sights nearby, and Stovepipe Wells is close enough to Furnace Creek to make a good spot from which to base your trip. Stovepipe Wells spots are first-come, first-served only.

Mesquite Springs (spur road left off Hwy. 190, south of Scotty's Castle, open year-round, $10) offers both tent and RV spots on the west side of Death Valley. It's the only campground in the high north country, near Scotty's Castle. It's a long drive to either Stovepipe Wells or Furnace Creek, the nearest spots that offer major services such as food and gasoline. But if you're specifically looking for isolation and a more rugged experience, Mesquite Springs might be just the place for you. It is first-come, first-served, with self registration, and the campground has potable water, flush toilets, and an RV dump station.

If you're willing to camp on the far west side of the park, **Panamint Springs** (Hwy. 190 past Western Entrance, west of Panamint Valley Rd., $15–30) offers a camping experience unique to all of Death Valley—that is, campsites along a river shaded by mature trees. No, really! One of the few year-round rivers in Death Valley runs and even cascades down a 20-foot fall about five miles back from the Panamint Springs Resort. With 40 RV spaces and 26 tent sites, call to make a reservation or arrive early in the morning if you want a spot in the winter months. You'll also find water and toilets throughout the campground, and 15 of the RV spots have full hookups with 50-amp electricity.

Tent-Only Campgrounds

If you want to camp Death Valley in the summertime, head up into the Panamint mountain range to the tent-only **Thorndike** (Mar.–Nov., free) campground. Be aware that you may need a four-wheel-drive vehicle to access this campground. Thorndike is a primitive campground, so you must bring all your own water for drinking and washing (bring lots more than you think you need to be safe). You will find pit toilets, and your site will include a picnic table and a fireplace. The nearby **Wildrose** (year-round, free) campground has a lower elevation and a wintertime crowd. It offers a few more in-season amenities, including potable water from November through April and a road you can drive in a passenger car. The nearest major services, such as food and gas, are a goodly drive to either Panamint Springs or Furnace Creek.

If you're into the western side of the park, consider camping at **Emigrant** (year-round, free), which sits about halfway between Panamint Springs and Stovepipe Wells. You'll get a spot to pitch your tent, access to potable water and flush toilets, but no fire rings here.

ACCOMMODATIONS
Under $100

If you prefer to stay on the west side of Death Valley (a good idea for at least one night if you're driving in from the California side), book a room or a camping spot at the tiny **Panamint Springs Resort** (Hwy. 190, 775/482-7680, www.deathvalley.com/psr, $89–170). This rustic lodge-style motel is the only independently owned lodging in Death Valley, and also has a temperature that's generally 10–15°F lower than the other motels in the park. Your amenities will not include a TV or much in the way of good phone service, but the resort does offer free Wi-Fi. You will have access to the resort's restaurant, which serves three meals a day year-round. If you're visiting in the wintertime and the weather is mild, get a seat out on the patio so you can enjoy a view of the valley with your food.

$100-250

The biggest resort complex in the park, **Furnace Creek Ranch** (Hwy. 190, 800/236-7916, www.furnacecreekresort.com, $135–225) acts as the human center of eastern Death Valley. It's in close proximity to many of the major attractions people come to see. If you stay here, you're on the same property as two restaurants, a tavern, a general store, a museum, a gas station, a golf course, an airstrip, and the main park visitors center. With a wide lawn, a playground, and a mineral spring–fed swimming pool, this is a great place to bring your kids for

Furnace Creek Ranch

a desert vacation. The guest accommodations at Furnace Ranch were deliberately created to be casual and, well, ranch-like. You can choose from standard, deluxe, or cabin-style accommodations. Rooms have one or two double or queen beds, chain-motel styling, and adequate bathroom facilities. Some rooms have tiny patios or balconies overlooking the lawns and pools. No smoking is permitted in any room.

The motel at **Stovepipe Wells** (Hwy. 190 past the big bend, 760/786-2387, www.stove pipewells.com, $135) offers basic rooms and amenities at reasonable prices. Choose between king or two-bed rooms, all ground floor rooms only a few steps from the restaurant and saloon, the swimming pool, and across the street from the general store. Your room will have a TV but no phone, beds with motel-style bedspreads and wall art, and a bathroom with a shower or tub combo— everything you'd expect (well, except the phone) from an inexpensive motel. From the motel, you'll have easy access to Mosaic Canyon, the local dunes, and Salt Creek.

Over $250

The lone high-end resort in all of Death Valley is the **Furnace Creek Inn** (Hwy 190. at Hwy. 178, 800/236-7916, www.furnace creekresort.com, $310–475, mid-Oct.–mid-May only). This beautiful property was constructed early in the 20th century by the Pacific Borax Company. It's a lovely place to come upon as you drive up Highway 190, with its palm oasis and multi-level adobe buildings rising up onto the hillside. As you pull up to the front of the hotel, you'll see the ingenious tunnels that perforate the complex, and the wonderful views out over the salt flats of southern Death Valley.

Inside, you might find your guest room a bit small given the price you're paying for it. The bathrooms are tiled and sparking clean, though the fixtures can be on the old side unless you're in a spa room. And not all rooms look out over the valley, so you might get a fabulous view of the Dumpsters in the back parking area. But the interior design is mellow and pleasant, with colors and patterns that

© LANCE SCOTT

the pool at Furnace Creek Inn

echo the desert outside. You've got a TV and a phone, room service, and access to all the lovely amenities the resort has to offer. Most rooms have king-sized beds and a couple of unique suites are available.

It's really those amenities you're paying so much for: the bathtub-warm mineral pool that's fed by a local hot spring and open late into the night, the poolside food service, the gazebo in the palm oasis, the fine dining room, spa services, and more. While you're visiting, be sure to take a leisurely tour of the property. The architecture and artwork are more than worth your time and attention. The staff, who take pains to provide every service a guest could ever want, will be happy to assist you in planning your park exploration as well.

FOOD

You'll need to plan your meals each day during your trip to Death Valley, since there are no fast food joints or 24-hour supermarkets where you can grab a quick bite at 4 P.M. or 4 A.M. In fact, Death Valley has no supermarkets or fast food, period. Either bring a cooler stocked with picnic supplies to carry with you each day as you explore the valley, or plan to be near one of the three resort areas at mealtimes. If you do plan to feed yourself, stock up on staples (particularly the nonperishable stuff like soda and water) outside the park to save money.

Casual Dining

If you're looking for a good, casual, diner-style meal, you won't do better in Death Valley than the **49er Café** (Hwy. 190 at Furnace Creek, 760/786-2345, daily until 9 P.M., $8–15) at the Furnace Creek Ranch. One of two restaurants on the property, the 49er Café is open the longest, serving a traditional American breakfast, filling lunches, and hearty dinners. While big eaters can get huge portions if they want them, it's a relief for the lighter eaters to find smaller items such as single eggs and half-grapefruits on the menu. The rustic dining room has some fun touches, including an original wood plank floor and plastic-covered maps of the valley on each table. You can plan out your day's travels

as you sit sipping your coffee and waiting for your eggs to arrive. The service staff gets the job done, and can be quite friendly especially if you choose a seat at the counter. Feel free to wear jeans and a T-shirt.

If you've burned untold hundreds of calories hiking around the valley during the day, you'll find the perfect replenishment at the **Wrangler Steakhouse** (Hwy. 190 at Furnace Creek, 760/786-2345, 6–9 A.M., 11 A.M.–2 P.M., 5–9 P.M., $23–35). The Wrangler offers a menu loaded with steaks, plus ribs and chicken smothered with tangy barbecue sauce. In the same weathered wooden structure with the 49er Café, you'll be treated to a casual atmosphere where you'll feel at home in jeans and boots. The short wine list includes a few California favorites. You can also grab a beer or a cocktail, and finish off your meal with a cappuccino or a latte. For breakfast and lunch, the Wrangler puts up a casual buffet with both hot and cold dishes.

If you're in the northern reaches of Death Valley around dinnertime, your option for a restaurant meal is the **Toll Road Restaurant** (Hwy. 190, Stovepipe Wells, 760/786-2387, www.stovepipewells.com, daily 7–10 A.M., 11:30 A.M.–2 P.M., and 5:30–9 P.M.). The Toll Road serves biscuits and gravy for breakfast, a burger for lunch, and some chicken or pasta for dinner. The small dining room manages to accommodate both the residents in the motel and the campground, plus the occasional tourist stopping in for lunch from another part of the park. But do be prepared to wait for a table on weekends in the high season.

The small size and lower traffic out west mean that the **Panamint Springs Resort Restaurant** (Hwy. 190 at west side of park, 775/482-7680, www.deathvalley.com/psr, $10–30) can serve home-cooked food to its diners all year long. Take a seat out on the large patio and enjoy a glass of beer before lunch or dinner—the restaurant offers more than 100 varieties from around the world.

Fine Dining

The few restaurants in Death Valley tend

toward solid American food with little frill or pretense. The only high-end dining establishment in the park is the **Furnace Creek Inn Dining Room** (Hwy. 190 at Hwy. 178, 760/786-3385, www.furnacecreekresort.com, Oct.–May, $18–30). Serving three meals per day to accommodate inn guests, the Dining Room offers large portions of delectable if sometimes a little bit overwrought California cuisine. Reservations are recommended for dinner, especially on weekend evenings. The servers make sure everything you need is taken care of in a timely fashion. Bring your appetite. The appetizers can be too tempting to resist, which might make the entrée and the luscious desserts seem a bit overwhelming. The lunch menu includes lighter but no less elegant fare, and breakfast is a reasonably standard California list of egg dishes and waffle-like things. The Dining Room bleeds elegance, with its white tablecloths and designer china. If you eat here in the daytime, you'll get a lovely view out towards the mountains from the picture windows. The Dining Room has a dress code, so be sure to bring at least one non-hiking outfit if you plan to dine here.

Markets

If you need groceries, you can buy them in two spots in Death Valley. The widest selection of food, drink, and goods is sold at the **Furnace Creek Ranch General Store** (Hwy. 190 at Furnace Creek Ranch). The exterior is quaint, but the interior is stuffed with shiny modern souvenirs. You can find clothes if you need them—even swimsuits! The food clusters at the back of the store, and you can get staples, drinks, milk, produce, and other perishables. The market also has ice cream and plenty of junk food.

Much smaller, but adequate in an emergency, is the **Stovepipe Wells General Store** (Hwy. 190 past the big bend at Stovepipe Wells). This store is more like an understocked mini-mart than a real general store, and more than half of the merchandise sold is souvenirs. You can buy water, soft drinks, and a few limited food items here, but don't plan to stock up since for that you must go to Furnace Creek or outside the park.

INFORMATION AND SERVICES

People can be lulled into a false sense of security because Death Valley is a national park. Yes, there are rangers here, and this is a geographically large park. But you are leaving civilization for real when you go to Death Valley. You can drive for miles without seeing another living soul, a telephone, or any means of assistance. Take some time to plan your trip to this enchanted but desolate region, making sure you've got lots of water (one full gallon per person, per day), a first-aid kit, a spare tire, and a good pair of walking shoes.

That said, most of the 1.2 million visitors who come to Death Valley each year have a fabulous time and no need to worry about the lack of nearby civilization.

Tourist Information

The main **Furnace Creek Visitors Center** (Hwy. 190, 760/786-3200, daily 9 A.M.–5 P.M.) sits just north of Furnace Creek Ranch. The rangers at this center tend to be experienced with the park and can give you good advice about the best spots to go at the best times. They'll also tell you where *not* to go. This visitors center also has a book and souvenir store, and an interpretive museum.

The other major in-park visitors center sits at **Scotty's Castle Visitor Center and Museum** (SR 267, 760/786-2392, summer daily 9 A.M.–4:30 P.M., winter daily 8:30 A.M.–5 P.M.). Here again you'll find an interpretive museum and rangers to help you with your itinerary. The bookshop is smaller, but an attached snack shop sells munchies and plenty of bottled water.

Media and Communications

Expect your cell phone to be out of commission for the whole of your stay in Death Valley. You might get lucky if you've got the right carrier, but most folks get no bars. Even many of the motels offer no in-room telephones, and most have little or no Internet access either. To come to Death Valley is to "disconnect" from modern communication gadgets almost completely. Some adults come here specifically for that reason, but be prepared for whining from older kids and teenagers when they discover they won't be able to text their friends for days at a time.

All the major resort areas have phones that can be used in an emergency, but you won't find any call boxes along the highway. Highway 190 has plenty of traffic traversing it every day—if you need to, you'll probably see plenty of cars and ranger trucks you can flag down for assistance. If you're serious about heading into Death Valley's back country, consider bringing a long-range, two-way radio just in case.

You can pick up a wealth of literature about the park from either visitors center. The major resort motels may offer the *LA Times*.

Medical Services

No significant medical services are available inside Death Valley. The closest hospital is **Barstow Community Hospital** (555 S. Seventh Ave., Barstow, 760/256-1761). On the Nevada side, contact the **Beatty Clinic** (775/553-2208) or the **Pahrump Urgent Care Facility** (775/727-6060).

GETTING THERE AND AROUND

A trip to Death Valley isn't like a trip to Los Angeles. The remote, harsh valley is surrounded by treacherous mountain ranges with few paved roads

Air

The closest major airport to Death Valley is the **Las Vegas International Airport** (5757 Wayne Newton Blvd., Las Vegas, 702/261-5211, www.mccarran.com). From Vegas, it's a two-to three-hour drive to Furnace Creek.

If you're lucky enough to have access to a light plane, you can fly right into the **Furnace Creek Ranch** (Hwy. 190, 760/786-2345, www.furnacecreekresort.com). The Ranch has an uncontrolled 3,000-foot runway with tie-down space for general aviators.

Car

The main north–south corridor through Death Valley is CA-190. CA-190 makes a hard turn to the west just before it passes through Stovepipe Wells and on out through Panamint Springs. Numerous paved, unpaved, and four-wheel-drive-only roads branch off from CA-190 throughout the park, letting visitors access the park's main attractions and trailheads.

THE HIGH PRICE OF GETTING STUCK

Before you visit Death Valley, check in with the rangers at the main visitors center (Furnace Creek, Hwy. 190, 760/786-3200, daily 9 A.M.–5 P.M.) to get up-to-the-minute information about the state of the four-wheel-drive roads in the park. Particularly at the north end of the park, razor-sharp volcanic rock can scatter across roads, not just cutting but actually shredding all but the heaviest duty all-terrain tires. The road to The Racetrack is the worst; it's not unusual for Hummers to lose more than one tire and end up stranded more than a dozen miles from the nearest paved road or source of help. Add to that the fact that most cell phones receive no signal anywhere in Death Valley, and you have a recipe for disaster.

So how do you extricate yourself from such a mess? You stay put, or walk out to the road until a park ranger comes to find you. The ranger will call the one and only tow company that makes runs out into Death Valley's backcountry. As the only game in town, this company happily charges whatever they want to help you. If they've got a spare tire or two in your size, the service might only cost you $800-1,000. But if you need a tow back to civilization, expect to shell out upwards of $2,000 for the privilege.

What's the moral of this story? Listen to the rangers if they tell you that a certain road is treacherous this season and consider carefully how much money you're willing to spend for your off-road adventure before you bump out beyond the reach of civilization.

To drive in to the park, you'll come either from NV-95 or CA-395, then turn off onto smaller roads that lead into the park. Get a map before you leave for the best navigation; GPS units also work in the park. The nearest major California town to Death Valley is Bakersfield. (Baker is closer, but it has fewer services.)

You'll need to keep an eye on your gas gauge and plan well when exploring Death Valley by car. Gas is available *only* at the resort areas of Panamint Springs, Stovepipe Wells, and Furnace Creek. In spring of 2008, the gas station at Scotty's Castle was not functional or open for business; check with the Park Service for an update before or during your visit.

Tours

It doesn't happen every year, but most years Death Valley receives just a very little bit of winter rainfall. When these miniscule rains bunch up, especially in January and February, the water is absorbed by the seeds of countless wildflowers. Come late February and March, these newly sprouted seeds grow up and then bloom, creating a stunning profusion of color spreading across the normally bleak and barren desert floor. The most prominent color you'll see is yellow, since the Desert Gold grows a foot or more tall and produces a brilliant golden daisy-like flower with an orange center. In amongst the gold you'll see streaks of purple, dots of pink, and puffs of white. In fact, flowers of every color in the rainbow grow in Death Valley when conditions are right.

The best way to see the flowers is to get out of your car and take a stroll out into the desert where they grow. Ironically, often the water vapor and carbon dioxide cars emit make the strips of land right beside the road the most colorful and prolific flowered areas. If you haven't studied botany recently and you'd like to know more about the beauty surrounding you, take a Wildflower Walk led by one of the park rangers during the season. Check with the Furnace Creek Visitors Center for a schedule of Walks.

Anza-Borrego Desert State Park

Anza-Borrego has a rich human history. Native Americans hunted bighorn sheep (still found here today) and gathered from the diverse plant life here, occasionally taking the time to draw and paint on the rocks. Later, European and Colonial explorers crisscrossed the desert with trails that you can still see traces of today.

The civilized center of the region is the town of Borrego Springs, a tiny patch of land that's not part of the state park. Most folks who come to enjoy the Borrego Desert's charms spend their nights here.

Many of the 600,000 acres of Anza-Borrego Desert State Park are pristine wilderness, yet camping is allowed anywhere in the park. Two of the best times to view the park as a whole are at sunrise and sunset. When the light is low and golden, the multicolored desert spreads out from the mountains to the south.

SIGHTS
Visitors Center

For first-time desert park visitors, a great place to start is the Visitors Center (200 Palm Canyon Dr., 760/767-4205, www.abdsp.org, Oct.–May daily 9 A.M.–5 P.M., June–Sept. weekends only). The Visitor Centers offers information, maps, trail updates, and interactive displays. An interpretive desert garden surrounds the center and provides the names and stories of many common plants and animals in the park. The stroll is easy and mostly flat, and includes a pupfish pond.

◖ Borrego Palm Canyon

If there's one natural feature you must see when you visit Anza-Borrego, it should be the Borrego Palm Canyon (spur road, just north of visitors center). An easy drive or walk from

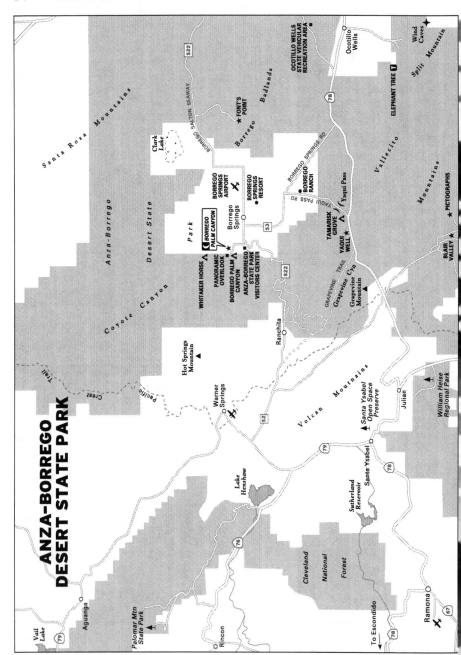

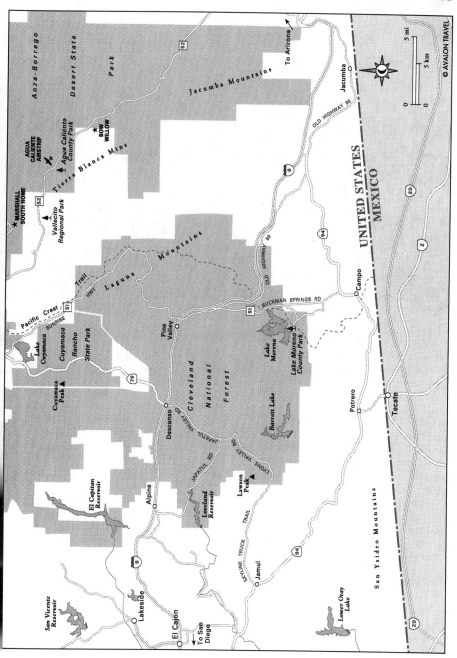

Anza-Borrego Desert State Park

© LIZ HAMILL SCOTT

the visitors center takes you to this surprising and lovely desert palm oasis. The best way to experience the canyon is to take the **Palm Canyon Nature Trail.** This three-mile loop trail takes you to the heart of the oasis, where you'll stand in a shady grove of fan palms beside the tiny creek that feeds them and the other plants whose precarious existence depend on its water. The palms you'll see are the only palm trees that are native to California. To learn more about the plants, rocks, former Native American residents, and animals that live here, pick up a trail guide from the visitors center.

Some visitors enjoy this hike and the surrounding region so much that they choose to camp at the foot of the canyon.

Panoramic Overlook

One of the many great views you can check out in Anza-Borrego sits between the visitors center and Borrego Palm Canyon. The Panoramic Overlook offers, well, a panoramic overlook of the desert stretching out to the east and down to the south. This is a wonderful place to take a camera or a folding chair at sunset on a clear day. The mountains turn all shades of blue, while the flat valley floor turns a light golden color with an occasional shimmering silver mirage for contrast. You can hike to the Panoramic Overlook from the Palm Canyon campground in about 1.5 miles. Expect to spend about an hour climbing up the somewhat steep hill, looking around, and walking back down. While this isn't the most strenuous trail in the park, it takes a little longer for visitors who aren't accustomed to hiking.

Yaqui Well

It's about 1.5-mile walk out from the road to the Yaqui Well (Yaqui Pass Rd. about 1 mile west of Hwy. 78 fork), which is a natural year-round spring that's supported the life closely surrounding it for centuries. The trailhead and campground sit just off Yaqui Pass Road/S-3 (they're the same road here), which heads from the Well past the unmissable Borrego Ranch and on into Borrego Springs. A trail guide from the visitors center to the north of town points out the interesting and in some cases unique features of the trail out to the spring, and of the spring itself. Because of the water, visitors get to see more abundant foliage and wildlife at Yaqui Well. Once upon a time, before conservation and state parks came along, ranchers actually grazed and watered cattle here. Before that, the Kumeyaay Native Americans camped here seasonally. Do be aware that any Kumeyaay artifacts you see lying on the ground are protected as part of the park—picking them up and taking them home is not only rude, it's actually illegal.

From the Yaqui Well trailhead you can also access the Cactus Loop Trail and the Tamarisk Campground, which has water and restroom facilities.

Font's Point

When you stand atop the visitors center or up on the Panoramic Overlook and gaze out east to see the funky rock formation that is Font's Point (Font's Wash, off the Borrego-Salton Seaway), it looks like it's only a mile or two away. Looks can be deceiving—especially in the desert where the clear, dry air distorts distances. It's actually about 10 miles from the visitors center in the Borrego Badlands. After you negotiate the four miles of dirt road (usually passable by passenger cars) and park in the dirt lot, you'll take a short walk up to Font's Point proper. From here, you'll get arguably the best look at the formation of the desert, from its time as lakes and marshes, ancient to current fault activity, uplift and drying, all the way to current washes and canyons created by flash floods and gradual erosion. Paleontologists come here to excavate fossils from the Pliocene and Pleistocene epochs—believe it or not, woolly mammoths once lived here! Font's Point makes for another great sunrise or sunset vantage point, and there's no sight in the world quite like that of the sun hitting the badlands.

Coyote Canyon

Coyote Canyon (entrances at the end of Horse Camp Rd. and DiGiorgio Rd.) encompasses the northernmost reaches of Anza-Borrego. Many seasonal creeks flow through this region during the flash-flood season, and the whole area is closed to human traffic from June through September to allow wildlife—especially the rare Borrego Bighorn Sheep—easy and fear-free access to the water here. Winter visitors can traverse the canyon's rough dirt roads in four-wheel-drive vehicles. Passenger cars can make it from the Borrego Springs Road cutoff up to Desert Gardens, but probably shouldn't try to go too far past due to deepening sand and rougher ruts.

Desert Gardens and the adjoining **Ocotillo Flats** offer some of the best cactus and ocotillo viewing in the whole of Anza-Borrego. Just park your car off to the side of the road (but not too far off—the sandy ground gets treacherously soft quickly!) and walk out into the desert to check out the variety of native plants that manage to thrive in this arid and inhospitable environment. The star of Ocotillo Flats gave the area its name and if you're there just after a rainstorm, you'll get to see the strangely beautiful ocotillos sprouting leaves and blooming. Ocotillos aren't cacti; they're a deciduous shrub that goes through a full cycle of leafing and dropping leaves each time it rains on the desert. It takes about a month for the new leaves to turn pretty colors and fall off, then the plant just sits and waits for the next rain. Out in the gardens, you'll find the misleadingly named teddy bear cactus (do not let your children hug them), the ubiquitous creosote bushes, wildflowers in the springtime, and all sorts of other desert cacti and plants.

One of the few leftovers of Anza-Borrego's years as ranchland is **Bailey's Cabin.** You can't reach the cabin from the 4WD road in Coyote Canyon. You'll have to park and hike several miles through desert sand out to the small but intact stone edifice. Originally used by the Bailey and Larner families as a line cabin on their ranch, today the state owns and maintains the cabin as part of the park. You can even camp inside it if you get there before anybody else claims it.

Blair Valley

Off the S-2 paved road you'll find the campground and attractions in and around Blair Valley (S-2 about 7 miles south of Hwy. 78). This central western region of the park offers any number of hiking trails, plus a high density of sights worth walking out to. If you're a big fan of Native American cultural archaeology, hike on out to the **pictographs,** figures painted by early residents of the desert. One big boulder contains all the artwork—mostly Kumeyaay girls' puberty drawings that formed part of the ritual that girls went through upon becoming adult women. Though the pictographs have faded severely in the harsh sunlight over the centuries, you can still see distinctive diamond chain patterns, intricate designs, shining suns, and other symbols.

For something different and yet rather similar, take the steep three-mile hike up to the remains of the **Marshall South Home** at the top of Ghost Mountain. Marshal and Tanya South were a couple ahead of their time, heading for the middle of the desert to live an anti-commercial, totally natural, and intensely difficult existence on a lonely desert peak. They raised three children in a small hilltop cabin without electricity, running water, or access to the modern world. Today, only the skeleton of the cabin remains for visitors to poke around in.

Split Mountain

At the eastern edge of the park, Split Mountain Road splits off from CA-78 and heads south toward the Fish Creek Mountains. It passes through the Ocotillo Wells recreation area to the north, then heads back into the park and terminates at the remains of an old **Gypsum Mine** (end of Split Mountain Rd.). From there, you can take the 4WD road out to the Split Mountain campground, or past it to the **Wind Caves** (about 5 miles south of Gypsum Mine). These are a cluster of sandstone boulders out of which the wind has carved holes, caves, and even arches over the centuries. While the formations aren't huge, they make a great place to enjoy lunch in the meager shade as the weather gets hot in the late spring and summertime. If you're visiting in the winter and looking for a walk, check out the **Elephant Tree Trail** (Split Mountain Rd., about 9 miles south of Hwy. 78) about midway down the paved road.

Bow Willow

Down at the south end of the park, the Bow Willow (S-2, about 20 miles north of I-8) region has both water and totally dry badlands topography.

If you take a fairly stout hike, you'll find the **Mountain Palm Springs.** Several springs feed palm oases and in one case a grove of the rare elephant trees. The moderate three-mile round-trip hike seems worth it when you get the chance to rest and relax in the natural shade of the tiny groves. Sit still enough and you might get to see some of the abundant wildlife coming out to drink from the year-round water sources.

Visitors more fascinated with the harsh side of the desert head for the **Carrizo Badlands Overlook.** From here you'll get to see old washes and ridges of rock that were originally deposited by a Colorado River that ran a very different course than the modern version does.

One attraction of this region that's changed recently is the **San Diego Imperial Railway.** The tracks, some of which run across amazing trestles, cross the southern tip of the park. *But,* unlike in previous years, walking the tracks and checking the tunnels is *not* a safe activity! The railroad, which lay dormant and essentially abandoned for years, now has trains running over it on a regular basis. The tunnels and trestles are especially dangerous for explorers, because there's no safe haven. The rails and their access are now private property of the railroad, and you can be ticketed (or worse) if you're found walking the tracks.

ENTERTAINMENT AND EVENTS

Anza-Borrego, similar to most desert parks, doesn't have too much in the way of happening nightlife. You can get a drink, though, if you're willing to do it fairly early in the evening. The **Krazy Coyote Saloon & Grille** (2220 Hoberg

Rd., Borrego Springs, 760/767-7788, www
.thepalmsatindianhead.com, daily 5 P.M.–close,
closed summer), despite its Western name, feels
more like a cocktail bar than a classic saloon.
Sure, they've got beer, but most guests at the
Krazy Coyote sip a nice California wine or
quaff a top-shelf margarita or a high-end vodka
martini. Call ahead to get the variable closing
time by season.

Another hotel bar worth looking into is
the **Hog Trough Cafe & Saloon** (221 Palm
Canyon Dr., Borrego Springs, 760/767-5341,
www.palmcanyonresort.com/saloon.htm, daily
5–10 P.M.). This saloon, with its oak bar and
eclectic decor, has more of the feel of a true
Western watering hole. The Hog Trough prides
itself on its Super Bowl party and its welcome
for two-wheeled desert travelers. So, bikers,
you've a friendly spot to show up, complete
with dedicated motorcycle parking.

SPORTS AND RECREATION

The outdoors calls to many visitors of Anza-
Borrego. Countless acres of unspoiled desert
are just waiting to be discovered by hikers, bikers, and riders. The Borrego Springs resorts
have a few golf courses and plenty of tennis
courts and swimming pools.

As always, it's important to remember that
when you go outside, you're entering a real
desert. It's hot, dry, dangerous, and remote.
People really can, and do, die out here every
year. Before you venture on even a moderate
hike or a flat-ish 4WD road, be sure you've
got plenty of water (up to one gallon per person per day), some snacks, sunscreen, a hat, a
map, and good walking shoes (even if you're
not walking right now, you never know when
you might have to). A first-aid kit, extra gas, a
spare tire, and a vehicle emergency kit might
also be a good idea.

The best time for outdoor recreation at
Anza-Borrego is from the fall through the
spring; temperatures are moderate and in the
spring the wildflowers bloom, adding to the
beauty of a hike or off-road trek. In the summertime, the dangerously high temperatures
make serious outdoor adventuring a bad idea.

Hiking

You can hike just about anywhere in the bounds
of Anza-Borrego State Park. If you want to, you
can just start at the visitors center and wander
straight off into the desert. On the other hand,
dozens of trails interlace the more visited and
accessible areas. Many hikes center around the
major sights in the park. Some of these trails
are more heavily maintained than others, but
don't expect pavement or boardwalks here. All
trails are primitive, and many get steep, rocky,
rough, sandy, or all of the above.

The **Bill Kenyon Overlook Trail** (Yaqui
Pass primitive camp, 1 mile round-trip, easy)
offers an easy walk in the **Tamarisk Grove
Area.** Shamble along, checking out the different kinds of cactus, before getting out to the
payoff-the view. You'll get a chance to look out
over the Pinyon Mountains, San Felipe Wash,
and other gorgeous features of the Anza-
Borrego desert.

A fascinating hike that shows off the best
of the Fish Creek Wash runs from **Mud Hills
Wash to Elephant Knees** (4.5 miles up Fish
Creek Rd. unpaved, off Split Mountain Rd.,
4 miles round-trip, moderate). Before you and
your ample supply of water set out, take a moment to read up on oyster shell reefs described
in the sign at the trail fork. The Fish Creek
Wash region was once a part of the long-gone
and dried up Gulf of California. You'll be seeing such reefs as you come upon the Mud Hills
Wash, and you'll even encounter loose shells
from more recent flooding. Once you've thor-
oughly explored the wash, it's time to climb
up the funky Elephant Knees Mesa. You'll be
tromping right up the oyster shell reef; in fact,
it's a good idea to watch your step here, because the loose shells can be hazardous. At the
top, hikers can look down and see the "knee"
formation of the bottom of the mesa. For the
best views on this hike, go at sunrise or towards sunset, when the lower sun limns the
layers of shells and ancient sediment in beautiful colors.

In the south of the park, the **Bow Willow**
region offers lots of great hiking, including
the network of trails in and around the oases

of the **Mountain Palm Springs.** The **North Fork** (2.5 miles, moderate) takes you on a good leg-stretching walk out to the Palm Bowl and Mary's Bowl Grove—a good place to see an elephant tree if you missed them to the north. The **South Fork** (3 miles, moderate) gets you to Pygmy Grove and the Totore Bowl. You can also walk the South Carrizo Creek road across S-2 and all the way out to the Carrizo Creek Wash if you're feeling energetic enough for a 20-mile round-trip trek!

For an easy and educational hike in the **Blair Valley** region, check out the **Trail to the Morteros** (unpaved Blair Valley Rd., 0.5 mile, easy). In less than an hour of easy walking, you'll get to see ancient grinding rocks used by local Native Americans to grind grains. The characteristic mortar-holes are all that remain of a once-industrious community here.

Horseback Riding

At Anza-Borrego, all the primitive roads open to 4WD vehicles and mountain bikes are also open to equestrian traffic. That makes more than 500 miles of trails to check out within the park boundaries. In addition, part of the **California Riding and Hiking Trail** (near the visitors center) runs through the park. You can also ride on the portion of the **Pacific Crest Trail** that passes through Anza-Borrego briefly at Granite Mountain. The PCT actually runs mostly parallel to and outside the western edge of the park.

Inside Anza-Borrego, one of the best-used trails is at **Coyote Canyon** in the northern reaches. Take care, and please don't let your horse trample the delicate landscape where the road tapers off. This is where you'll find the Vern Whitaker Horse Camp, with its corrals making a desert trip with your horse both possible and comfortable. Another stand-out riding road is the **Jasper Trail** (15 miles) that runs through Grapevine Canyon in the middle western section of the park.

Didn't bring your own horse to Anza-Borrego? You can take a two-hour ride on one of the few and extremely well-tended Arabians of the **Smoketree Arabian Ranch** (302 Palm Canyon Dr., 866/408-1812, www.smoketree arabianranch.com, $95/person). This isn't your typical meat-grinding rental ranch. Yu'll find no sad, tired old nags wearing their saddles all day here. Instead, your ride will include grooming and preparing your mount as you get to know him or her before you ever climb into the saddle. You and your horse will enjoy learning about one another as you take a ride out into the beautiful desert landscape. Serious equestrians will love the way the folks at Smoketree take care of their beloved horses. But because there are few of them available for "guest" rides, be sure to call in advance to make reservations. The spring wildflower season is the busiest for Smoketree.

Golf

Yes, there is golfing even out here in this wild desert country. The "premier" local courses sit on the land of the **Borrego Springs Resort** (1112 Tilting T Dr., 760/767-3330, www.borrego springsresort.com, greens fees $40–65, cart included). You'll find three separate nine-hole courses: The Palms, Desert Willow, and Mesquite. Pick any two to create an 18-hole day. Or take advantage of the short, cool mornings for a quick nine holes before the desert really heats up. Borrego Springs also has practice facilities, a pro shop, and regularly scheduled tournaments. Check the website for hotel-and-golf packages, as well as year-round lessons and clinics to improve your game.

Another great nine-hole course in the Borrego Springs region is **The Springs at Borrego** (2255 DiGiorgio Rd., 866/330-0003, www .springsatborrego.com/golf.htm). The Springs is adjacent to the RV park that goes by the same name. At a par-36 with a practice range, this small but technical course is perfect for golfers who want a challenging but not too-long day on a desert course. For golfers who've come to the desert specifically to play the game, there's also the **RoadRunner Golf Course** (1010 Palm Canyon Dr., 760/767-5374, www.roadrunner club.com/golf). This short 18-hole, par-3 course is great for newer golfers while helping more experienced players improve their short game.

Off-Roading

Anza-Borrego State Park offers over 500 miles of dirt and sand roads accessible by highway-legal four-wheel-drive vehicles. These run around almost all areas of the park, letting you explore many places that are inaccessible otherwise. So bring your favorite tagged boonie-crasher and have a blast!

The **Jasper Trail & Grapevine Canyon** (access via Jasper Trail of S22, 13.5 miles, easy to moderate) offers a graded trail for most of the ride. You can stop and see some rare desert water welling up from Stuart Spring. Take a left here to remain on the trail and go toward the Yaqui Well primitive campground, or a right to head back out to Highway 78. If you pass Yaqui Well and head out onto the *bajada*, you'll get to see some lovely cactus varieties alongside the trail.

Want to feel like a serious boonie-crasher? Take the **Fish Creek Trail** (easy to moderate). You'll first find yourself bumping along a fault on a fairly wide track. Extremely primitive camping (no restrooms) is available at Fish Creek. From here, the trail narrows into Fish Creek Canyon, where you'll get to see the famous oyster reef cliffs. *Don't* take the Arroyo Seco del Diablo cutoff, since it's got a nasty drop that makes it dangerous to drive from this direction. Instead, keep going toward the **Sandstone Canyon Trail** (moderate to difficult). Here you'll get a great experience: tight maneuvering through narrow canyons of wind-eroded soft sandstone.

Pinyon Mountain Road (end of Big Rock Creek Rd., 7 miles plus 4-mile spur, easy to moderate) crosses in and out of the state park and starts close to Camp Fenner State Prison—so don't pick up any hitchhikers here! You'll get a good mix of open trail driving and creek fording, and on the spur road you can head up for a view of Devil's Punchbowl and Big Rock Creek and even on into a pine forest. Lots of out-of-the-car activities stem from this road, including access to the Pacific Crest Trail for hikers and deer hunting on the U.S. Forest Service land.

Longing for a glimpse of another country? Take the **Calcite Mine Trail** (S22 18.5 miles east of Borrego Springs, difficult). You'll bump up a difficult and slick trail (take care and use a spotter) that will take you up to a ridge that lets you look south toward Mexico. From there, the road gets even bumpier and more boulder-filled, so consider hoofing it the rest of the way to the abandoned calcite mine. When you get there, look but don't take; it's illegal to remove calcite crystals from the State Park.

While Anza-Borrego has many primitive roads worth checking out in your (mandated by the park) street-legal, possibly four-wheel-drive vehicle, the park might not make for your idea of great four-wheeling fun. Right next door, so to speak, sits the immense **Ocotillo Wells State Vehicular Recreation Area** (760/767-5391, ohv.parks.ca.gov, year-round, free). Countless (well, 80,000) acres of desert have been set aside specifically for boonie-crashers to test the mettle of their baddest trucks and best dirt bikes. Bring your rock-crawling 4WDs, open dune buggies, and other toys. Tags aren't required here. You can camp for up to 30 days, but you must bring your own water, as *no water is available inside the park.*

Be aware that Ocotillo Wells is immensely popular, and 4WD lovers come from all over California to drive here. If you're planning to visit on a holiday weekend, expect severe traffic congestion (especially when leaving) and crowding on the trails and in the camping areas.

Biking

You're welcome to break out your mountain bike and bump along any of the primitive roads in Anza-Borrego, some of which are sandy, rough, and steep. However, no bikes are permitted on hiking trails or overland off the roads. Check out adjoining Ocotillo Wells for more extreme mountain biking opportunities.

CAMPING

Anza-Borrego is the only state park in the California system to allow camping anywhere within its boundaries. For real. Just pull your car off the road and tromp off into the desert with your tent, find a big rock, and pitch your tent in its shadow. The catch? You'll need to take care of yourself out in the unrelenting desert. No bathrooms, no water, no nothing—just you and a shovel. If you want a more civilized desert camping experience, pick one of the RV-friendly campgrounds or even the minimally developed backcountry campgrounds.

Developed Campgrounds

Few well-developed campgrounds grace the parched lands of Anza-Borrego. But if you really want an RV slot or a tent site with access to flush toilets and showers, you can find one. For the developed campgrounds, be sure to make a reservation in advance at 800/444-7275. Nearest to the visitors center you can stay at the **Borrego Palm Canyon Campground.** This large and somewhat desolate campground has over 100 campsites, 55 with RV hookups. (Call ahead to see if the dump station is functioning before your visit.) In addition to the showers and restrooms, working phones are available here. Some campsites have fire rings.

The **Tamarisk Grove Campground** (Road S-3 and Hwy. 78, $10–15) has 27 RV sites with access to showers, toilets, and phones. It is the southernmost fully developed campground in Anza-Borrego.

For equestrians, Anza-Borrego maintains the **Vern Whitaker Horse Camp** (Horse Camp Rd., $16). Forty corrals lie adjacent to 10 campsites, making it possible for campers to sleep near their horses. Though running water and full bathrooms grace the campground, the showers are solar heated so you may be taking a chance by using them.

Primitive Campgrounds

Plenty of primitive campgrounds dot the land of Anza-Borrego. Also, you're permitted to camp anywhere in the park. Just be sure you've got the equipment and supplies you'll need before you pull off at your favorite cactus garden and pitch your tent. (Remember: There are no bathrooms out in the middle of the desert!) Most of the primitive campgrounds have pit or chemical toilet facilities and very little else in the way of amenities. Camping at either the primitive campgrounds or off in the rocks and sands is usually free.

The campgrounds at **Culp Valley, Yaqui**

Pass, and **Arroyo** have reasonable access to paved roads. From dirt roads (most accessible via passenger cars), you can get to the sites at **Fish Creek, Yaqui Well, Blair Valley,** and **Bow Willow.** Bow Willow has more sites than most, takes reservations, and has a $7–9 per night fee. If you're interested in solitude and silence, and you're up for a hike in to your campsite, you might consider the sites at **Marshall South Home** and **Sheep Canyon.**

ACCOMMODATIONS

Many visitors to the desert prefer not to experience its harsh beauty 24 hours a day. For them, the town of Borrego Springs, which sits right in the middle of the park, offers a wide range of motels and resorts to suit every taste and budget range.

Under $100

The **Stanlunds Resort Inn and Suites** (2771 Borrego Springs Rd., 760/767-5501, www .stanlunds.com, $62–175) offers a convenient motel room at the right price for desert rats on a budget. Nope, it's not much to look at, but the guest rooms are reasonably clean, the beds are comfortable, and the bathroom plumbing works most of the time. You'll find the rooms rather small and decorated in standard motel florals and dark carpets, many with at least one white-painted brick wall. Larger rooms have dining areas and some have kitchens and patios as well. An outdoor pool beckons to guests who need to cool off after a long day exploring the desert, and the location downtown makes it great for dining and shopping in Borrego Springs.

$100-150

For affordable luxury on your desert vacation, get a room at the **Borrego Springs Resort** (1121 Tilting T Dr., 760/767-5700, www.borrego springsresort.com, $115–200). Spacious rooms include comfortable modern wood-framed beds, fine cotton bedding, big bathrooms, and pretty views of mountains or the pool areas. For multiple rooms and a kitchenette, choose one of the suites. Decor tends toward the simple motel style, with quiet soothing colors. Outside of your room, take a dip in one of the two pools or lounge beside them in a covered cabana to keep the sun off. One of the biggest attractions of the resort is the attached country club golf course; check the website for packages. You can also play tennis, or ask at the desk about guided tours of Anza-Borrego State Park. Plenty of dining is available on-site, from the fancy white tablecloths at The Arches dining room to the casual Roadrunner Café. If you just want a nice before or after dinner drink, take a seat beside the column-shaped fireplace and order a classic cocktail.

$150-250

For some travelers, it's important that their motel match with the nature and culture of its surroundings. The **Borrego Valley Inn** (405 Palm Canyon Dr., 800/333-5810, www .borregovalleyinn.com, $195–300) does just that, with low, blocky, orange adobe-style buildings with red tile roofs, and desert garden landscaping throughout. Wander the grounds,

or just sit on a wooden bench and watch the birds hop about enjoying the flowers and bugs. If you're serious about your nature loving, you can take a skinny-dip in the clothing-optional swimming pool and spa (privacy fenced for everyone's comfort, and directly accessible from rooms 1–7).

Even the smallest rooms are characteristic of its charm. All guest rooms have red-tiled floors, desert floral or Native American–inspired bedspreads and decor, matching accent decorations, cable TV, patios, and nice bathrooms. Bigger rooms might have gas fireplaces, walk-in showers, or soaking tubs, while all rooms have fridges, microwaves, and coffee makers. The largest suite offers a full homey kitchen, one bedroom, and stunning tile work.

Over $250

For the big spenders who want the beauty of the desert without any of its discomforts, there's **Borrego Ranch Resort & Spa** (3845 Yaqui Pass Rd., Borrego Springs, 800/824-1884, www.borregoranch.com, $400–1,700). This

© LANCE SCOTT

Borrego Ranch Resort & Spa

great sprawling resort has everything a luxury vacationer could ever need or want for a night, a week, or a month in Anza-Borrego. The recreation facilities include tennis courts, a state-of-the-art fitness center, an archery range, a tournament croquet field, and no fewer than five swimming pools. Families can enjoy pools designated just for them, complete with complimentary toys, while adults can relax or exercise in peace at the adults-only pools and spas. If you're renting one of the casitas, you may have your own private large spa or small swimming pool.

Nineteen such casitas grace the property, and they're more the size and shape of comfortable small homes than hotel rooms. You can bring your family and friends to share the comfy multiple bedrooms, beautiful desert-themed decor, and top-shelf amenities of these detached houses. Even the regular poolside rooms (yup, they're all poolside) offer tremendous space, cushy furniture, spacious bathrooms, and all the wonderful extras Borrego Ranch lavishes upon its guests to justify the lavish prices. Each room includes a full breakfast in the dining room each day.

Another reason to spend all that money on your lodgings here is the service—from the dining room to the desk staff to the fitness attendants, most everyone at Borrego Ranch will go out of their way to help you. If you need advice on activities either inside or outside the resort, they can definitely hook you up.

FOOD
Casual Dining
Looking for a tasty breakfast or lunch? Try locals' favorite **(** **Red Ocotillo** (2220 Hoberg Rd., Borrego Springs, 760/767-7400, daily 7 A.M.–9 P.M., $10–20). Despite the exotic desert name, this friendly and welcoming restaurant serves up classic diner food. Just look for the Palms at Indian Head. The interior dining room is done in retro-American kitsch, while the small outdoor dining area lets diners with dogs eat in the company of their canine friends. You'll find the service good even when there's a crowd, but the real

reason to come to Red Ocotillo is the food. Diners rave about the simple but delectable fresh biscuits and gravy, served all day along with the rest of the breakfast menu. Lunch and dinner items run to classic American staple entrées, sandwiches, and so on. For a great inexpensive meal in the desert, Red Ocotillo is your best bet.

After hours out in the southwestern desert scenery of Anza-Borrego, a Mexican dinner seems like the perfect way to end the day. **Pablito's of The Desert** (590 Palm Canyon Drive, Borrego Springs, 760/767-5753, daily 11 A.M.–2:30 P.M., 5–9 P.M., $5–15) offers good solid Mexican staples with a little bit of a desert twist—such as cactus in a breakfast egg dish. Yes, they serve breakfast even though Pablito's doesn't open until later in the morning. You'll also find extremely tasty lunch and dinner options.

Fine Dining
For an upscale meal in the low desert, you can't beat the **Cimarrón Room** at Borrego Ranch (3845 Yaqui Pass Rd., Borrego Springs, 800/824-1884, www.borregoranch.com, daily 7–11 A.M. and 11:30 A.M.–3:30 P.M., dinner nightly, $25). True, it has the advantage of being pretty much the top game in a small town, but you'll still find a low-lit, rambling dining room with a charming romantic atmosphere. Or ask for a table out on the patio on the endless warm desert evenings. The service can be variable, but the quality of the innovative dishes remains constant here. Look for high-end California stylings, including organic and sustainable produce and meat. The wine list is a star, and you'll find a long, long list of California and European wines. For a special treat, try a different glass with each course, including dessert.

The **Krazy Coyote Saloon & Grille** (2220 Hoberg Rd., Borrego Springs, 760/767-7788, www.thepalmsatindianhead.com, opens daily at 5:30 P.M., closed during summer, $20–40) is a Borrego Springs favorite. The the entrées are interesting and the homemade complimentary breads and "nibbles" make diners feel pampered. Visitors enjoy the casual-elegant atmosphere with windows overlooking the resort pool. Do expect to pay handsomely for the privilege of eating here, but most diners feel that the experience (and the martinis) are worth it.

Markets

Need to stock up on groceries before a camping stint out in the park? Head for the **Center Market** (590 Palm Canyon Dr., # 304, Borrego Springs, 760/767-3311, Mon.–Sat 8:30 A.M.–6:30 P.M., Sun. 8:30 A.M.–5 P.M.) for the basics. For good fresh produce, join the locals at the **Borrego Springs Farmers' Market** (Christmas Circle and Palm Canyon Dr., Borrego Springs, Fri. 7 A.M.–noon) on Friday mornings. Grapefruit are the specialty of the region, so be sure to pick up some of the local Borrego breed if you can. They're sweet and pink and juicy.

INFORMATION AND SERVICES

The only town within an easy distance of the park is Borrego Springs. It's not a one-streeter, but Borrego Springs is definitely a small town, so don't expect all the services and conveniences of a major city here.

Tourist Infomation

The **Anza-Borrego State Park Visitors Center** (200 Palm Canyon Dr., 760/767-4205, www.abdsp.org, Oct.–May daily 9 A.M.–5 P.M., June–Sept. weekends only) sits right outside of town, beyond an odd little turnoff near the end of Palm Canyon Road. It includes a ranger station, an interpretive display area, and a demonstration desert garden outside and on its roof. Rangers here can help you plan drives and hikes, and give you advice on the best places for views, wildflowers, and wildlife.

Media and Communications

The Internet and cell phone towers have come to Borrego Springs. Many of the resorts and motels offer Wi-Fi (sometimes free, sometimes not). Cell service is easy to come by in town, but can get spotty as you get farther out into the park. Don't expect your cell phone to save you if you get trapped in the badlands—have plenty of supplies on hand in case of emergency.

The **Borrego Sun** is the local paper, available in newspaper stands outside the Center Market.

Medical Services

The nearest major hospital to Anza-Borrego with an emergency room is the **John F. Kennedy Memorial Hospital** (47111 Monroe St., Indio, 760/347-6191, www.jfkmemorial hosp.com), 34 miles away in Indio. The **Borrego Medical Clinic** (4343 Yaqui Pass Rd., 760/767-5051) is open 8:30 A.M.–5 P.M. on weekdays only. They do have a 24-hour answering service that can get you in touch with a doctor if you need to ask a medical question.

GETTING THERE AND AROUND
Air

The closest commercial airports to Anza-Borrego are the **San Diego International Airport** (3665 N. Harbor Drive, San Diego, 619/400-2400 www.san.org) and the **Palm Springs International Airport** (3400 E. Tahquitz Canyon Way, Palm Springs, 760/318-3800, www.palmspringsairport.com). There is a private airport three miles east of **Borrego Springs** (1820 Palm Canyon Dr., 760/767-7415).

Car

Anza-Borrego State Park sits about an hour from Palm Springs to the north and from San Diego to the west. The major east–west road through the park is CA-78. County roads S-2 and S-3 run north and south through the desert, and S-22 heads east out of Borrego Springs toward CA-86.

On holiday weekends and popular spring Sundays, traffic can get very heavy on Highway 78 to the adjoining Highway 79 leaving the park to the west. Expect to creep along, possibly for hours, and plan extra time and maybe a food stop on the way out.

While you can get around the park in a passenger car, if you want to explore the dirt roads of the back country in-depth, you'll need a four-wheel-drive vehicle. Check with park rangers about current road conditions.

Tours

Anza-Borrego has a long wildflower season, which can run from January all the way through April in moister years. Check with the state park headquarters (760/767-4684, www.parks.ca.gov) for annual wildflower predictions and status reports. You can also either call or check in at the ranger station for information on guided wildflower tours during your stay.

JULIAN

Between San Diego and Anza-Borrego State Park sits the tiny mining town of Julian. When gold fever struck California, it quickly spread throughout the whole huge territory—even this far south. But if you've been exploring the small towns of Gold Country proper, you're in for a shock when you enter the town limits of Julian. This is a Gold Town, complete with endless crowds and parking nightmares. Residents of both San Diego and Los Angeles escape to the small-town atmosphere of Julian, with its cute shops and many public events, almost every weekend of the year.

Sights

Most folks who come to Julian spend their time walking up and down the sidewalks of **Historic Downtown Julian.** With its many shops and restaurants, pretty old-style buildings, and attractive woodsy setting, Downtown Julian makes a nice change from the arid valleys all around it. Expect a crowd, but you'll still enjoy a stroll downtown.

Believe it or not, you can actually go wine-tasting in Julian. **Orfila Vineyards** (4470 Hwy. 78, Julian, 760/765-0102, www.orfila wines.com, Wed.–Mon. 10 A.M.–5 P.M.) has a notable reputation throughout the state. They're famous for their Rhone wines, including Viognier, Marsanne, and perhaps most of all Syrah. Their cooler weather varietals come from vineyards in coastal California. Orfila's other tasting room sits in the San Pasqual Valley north of San Diego.

The **Witch Creek Winery** (2000 Main St., Julian, 760/765-2023, www.witchcreekwinery .com, daily 11 A.M.–5 P.M.) has a fabulous long list of red wines, a few whites, and a fun cat theme running through their labels. You'll find some fascinating and unusual wines here. Ever tasted a Montepulciano before? How about an Aglianico? Witch Creek also offers a delicious array of red blends, and even a hard apple cider. Whatever your tastes, you'll find something to love at this fabulous small winery. Check out Carlsbad for the winery's other tasting room.

Accommodations

If the heat of the desert in Anza-Borrego gets to you after a while, Julian can make a nice cool base of operations to escape back to after a day of desert explorations. Lodgings in Julian run to rustic B&Bs and vacation cabin rentals in the woods outside of town.

For a reasonably priced, rustic room in Julian, stay at the **Angels Landing Country Inn and Resort** (2323 Farmer Rd., Julian, 760/765-2578, www.angelresort.com, $90–160). Angels Landing offers quite a few family- friendly rooms and suites with multiple beds per room. Rooms fairly small with cute decor. The Lilac Building can sleep up to 10 people. The best part about this lodging is the setting—outside of town in the meadows and forested mountainside.

The **Butterfield Bed & Breakfast** (2284 Sunset Dr., Julian, 760/765-2179, www.butter fieldbandb.com, $135–185) is just as cute and country-kitsch as Julian itself. Each of the five rooms has unique decor, from elegant antique European to patchwork-quilted country Americana. All rooms have private bathrooms and cable TV, and the large private cottage can sleep up to four for an additional fee (all other rooms sleep two). Guest rooms come with a full breakfast each morning, served outdoors in the gazebo in summer and inside by the fire in winter.

A nod to luxury in Julian, **Orchard Hill Country Inn** (2502 Washington St., Julian, 760/765-1700, www.orchardhill.com, $210–500) offers 22 elegant guest rooms in a serene garden setting. Expect elegant updated decor and appointments, complete with lovely tiles, restored antique furniture, and a homelike clutter of linens and pillows. Some cottage rooms have whirlpool tubs, and all cottages have patios or porches for summer lounging and fireplaces for winter snuggling. All guests receive a full breakfast, afternoon nibbles and wine (or beer), and upscale amenities.

For a more independent lodging experience, Julian's many vacation cabin rentals are a great choice. The **Artists' Loft, Big Cat Cabin,** and **Strawberry Hill Cabin** (4811 Pine Ridge Ave., Julian, 760/765-0765, www.artistsloft.com, $195) are all managed by the same folks. Each cabin is unique, but all share a combination of rustic construction and decoration juxtaposed with comfortable amenities. Expect to find a large sitting room with fireplace, a full kitchen with a few basic staples provided, a separate comfortable bedroom with season-appropri-ate bedding, and a porch or window-seat area. You're welcome to bring a full supply of grocer-ies and cook for yourself throughout your stay at any of the cabins.

Food

The acknowledged favorite pie shop in town is **Mom's Pie House** (2119 Main St., Julian, 760/765-2472, www.momspiesjulian .com, Mon.–Fri. 8 A.M.–5 P.M., Sat.–Sun. 8 A.M.–6 P.M., $10). Naturally, the specialty of the house is old-fashioned apple pie. You'll also find crumb-crust pies, apple-boysenberry, apple-cherry, strawberry rhubarb, and more pie flavors. If you can't take a whole pie, just stop in for a slice of your favorite flavor, maybe topped with ice cream or real whipped cream. You can also grab a sandwich and a cup of cof-fee while you're here. Expect crowds and lines on holiday and event weekends.

For a full meal, check out the **Julian Grille** (2224 Main St., Julian, 760/765-0173, daily 11 A.M.–3 P.M., Tues.–Sun. 5–9 P.M., $10–20), which serves higher-than-expected quality seafood and steaks in a quaint cot-tage. Another American diner-style eatery is the **Cowgirl Café** (2116 Main St., Julian, 760/765-2167, $10–20). The kitsch factor gets high in this tiny eatery—check out the cowgirl memorabilia on the walls. But the

main reason to brave the lines at this eight-table restaurant is the quality of the food. Expect salads to be fresh, sandwiches bal-anced and tasty, and desserts to be made with local apples (of course). Despite the oft-crowded dining room and small staff, service is both friendly and fast, prompting locals to give their names and wait up to 30 minutes for a table on weekends. Call for the current operating hours.

Romano's Dodge House (2718 B St., Julian, 760/765-1003, www.romanosjulian .com, Wed.–Mon. 11:30 A.M.–8:30 P.M., $18) is billed as the most romantic restaurant in Julian. Certainly it's cute, with its red-checked tablecloths and soft mood lighting. But what's really delightful here is the food. Sure, you can get a good bowl of pasta or a pizza but even better are the specialty entrées—unique dishes made with local ingredients (yes, apples and cider) that combine an Italian aesthetic with California creativity. The wine list features local Julian vintages as well as wines from around California and imported from Italy. Reservations are recommended for dinner, es-pecially on weekends in fall and winter. Oh, and bring cash, as Romano's does not accept credit cards.

Practicalities

The **Julian Chamber of Commerce** (2129 Main St., 760/765-1857, www.julianca.com, daily 10 A.M.–4 P.M.) consists of a tiny office and a big rack of brochures. You'll find al-most everything you need in the brochures, including over a dozen possible places to stay overnight.

Julian lies at the junction of CA-78 and CA-79. You can drive there from Anza-Borrego in the east or San Diego to the west. Because Julian is incredibly popular as a weekend get-away destination, parking on Main Street can be challenging. You'll probably need to find parking on a side street two or three blocks from the action. During events, signs and townsfolk can help guide you to dirt lots (which you'll have to pay to use) near but not in of the center of town.

MOON PALM SPRINGS
Avalon Travel
a member of the Perseus Books Group
1700 Fourth Street
Berkeley, CA 94710, USA
www.moon.com

Editor: Sabrina Young
Series Manager: Kathryn Ettinger
Copy Editor: Ellie Behrstock
Graphics Coordinator: Elizabeth Jang
Production Coordinator: Elizabeth Jang
Cover Designer: Stefano Boni
Map Editor: Albert Angulo
Cartographers: Chris Markiewicz, Kat Bennett,
   Jon Niemczyk, Brice Ticen
Cartography Director: Mike Morgenfeld

ISBN-13: 978-1-59880-356-3

Front cover photo: Sunset in Joshua Tree National
Park © Laurin Rainder/dreamstime.com
Title page photo: Anza-Borrego State Park, Metal
Horses by Sculptor Ricardo Breceda, photo ©
Sabrina Young,

Printed in United States

ABOUT THE AUTHOR

Liz Hamill Scott

Liz Hamill Scott was born and raised in the San Francisco Bay Area. After getting her English degree at local institution Stanford University, she pursued her love of dining and travel throughout the golden state and beyond. Her exploits included everything from whitewater rafting on the Kaweah River to dining at the French Laundry. When a battle with chronic pain put an end to her rafting and camping trips, Liz discovered wine tasting and spa resorts. To this day, she's not sure which style of vacation she likes better.

In 2008, she made the terrifying leap from overpaid high-tech employee to almost broke full-time freelance travel and food writer. Exploring Southern California's deserts to write *Moon Palm Springs* gave Liz the chance to fall in love with her home state all over again. You can read about her adventures in national magazines, Bay Area newspapers, and on the web at www.liz-scott.com.

Liz lives and writes, often chasing her cats away from her computer so she can get some work done, in San Jose.